THE SEASONS

THE SEASONS

An exploration of twelve country walks

Watercolours by Liz Butler

Text by Michael Chinery

COLLINS   St James's Place, London   1982

The publication of this book has been made possible by sponsorship from Gulf Oil Corporation

For John

William Collins Sons & Co Ltd
London · Glasgow · Sydney · Auckland
Toronto · Johannesburg

British Library Cataloguing in Publication Data

Chinery, Michael

The Seasons
1. Great Britain—Description and travel—1971—Guide-books
I. Title   II. Butler, Liz
914.1'04858   DA632

ISBN 0—00—216319—5

First published 1982
© in the illustrations Liz Butler 1982
© in the text Michael Chinery 1982

Designed by Marian Morris
Photoset in Spectrum
Made and printed by W S Cowell Ltd, Ipswich, Suffolk

CONTENTS

Introduction 6

Spring

Summer

Autumn

Winter

INTRODUCTION

Our aim in this book has been to capture in words and pictures some of the moods and essences of Britain's countryside and wildlife, as observed on twelve monthly walks, taken in widely scattered parts of the country. The areas have been chosen to cover as wide a variety of landscape and habitat as possible, and also to take in some of Britain's rich history; while the season for each walk has been carefully selected to demonstrate the full richness of the annual cycle of the seasons – the gradual awakening of life in the spring, the blossoming of colour in the summer and autumn, and the subsequent slowing down in the face of the winter cold.

The 90,000 square miles that make up the land of Britain form no more than a small spot on the surface of the globe, but they present a remarkable kaleidoscope of scenery. In a single day's drive of perhaps 300 miles it is possible to see flat coastal marshes, rolling chalk downs, broad river valleys, rugged mountains, and precipitous sea cliffs. Taller mountains, broader rivers, and more extensive plains can be found in many other countries, but few other areas of comparable size can match Britain's great variety. A look at a geological map will reveal the reason for the quick-fire changes in landscape, for rocks of virtually every age and type are exposed somewhere in Britain. Many of the outcrops form bands just a few miles across. A journey from the North West Highlands to the Thames Estuary will take you over all of the major rock strata, representing a journey through geological time of about 3000 million years. The oldest rocks are in the north and the west and, because these also tend to be the hardest rocks, they form most of the high ground. Softer rocks, which are more easily eroded by the forces of nature, make up the lowlands of the south and east.

As well as creating scenery, the underlying rocks have a profound effect on natural history, and it is very often possible to identify the rocks of a region just by looking at its vegetation. Lowland heaths, for example, are indicative of sandstones, while ashwoods tell us that the rocks are limestones

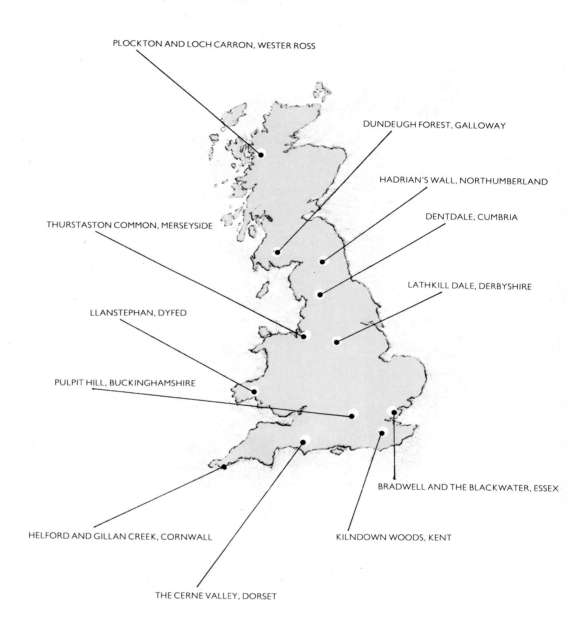

PLOCKTON AND LOCH CARRON, WESTER ROSS

DUNDEUGH FOREST, GALLOWAY

HADRIAN'S WALL, NORTHUMBERLAND

DENTDALE, CUMBRIA

THURSTASTON COMMON, MERSEYSIDE

LATHKILL DALE, DERBYSHIRE

LLANSTEPHAN, DYFED

PULPIT HILL, BUCKINGHAMSHIRE

BRADWELL AND THE BLACKWATER, ESSEX

HELFORD AND GILLAN CREEK, CORNWALL

KILNDOWN WOODS, KENT

THE CERNE VALLEY, DORSET

and pedunculate oakwoods indicate heavy clay. In Britain, within the limitations imposed by our climate, we have just about every possible habitat or biotope. Obviously we have no deserts, permanent ice-caps, or tropical forests, but we do have grasslands, heathlands and moorlands, lakes and rivers, coniferous forests, deciduous forests, and several thousand miles of extremely variable coastline with sand dunes, saltmarshes, and cliffs of all kinds. In addition, there are the vast acreages of highly modified agricultural land with its mosaics of fields and walls or hedgerows. Very little of Britain's countryside can be regarded as completely natural: apart from some of the highest mountain tops and certain coastal regions, all the land has been changed by human activity during the last two thousand years. The natural vegetation for most of the country is forest, but very little of the original forest cover remains and, wild as they might seem, the downs and moorlands are really only semi-natural communities.

Superimposed on the various landscapes and habitats are the far-reaching seasonal changes, which can totally transform an area within days. This was forcefully demonstrated during the preparation of this book when October gales removed virtually all the colour from the Chiltern beechwoods in three days. Thanks to our island position and Atlantic climate, our weather is also notoriously variable – 'If you don't like the British weather, just wait a minute' runs one music-hall joke – and these variations can quickly change the 'mood' as well as the appearance of the landscape. A few clouds can transform a whole scene by altering the pattern of light and shade, and the ultimate change comes when the clouds bring snow. This, too, was vividly demonstrated as we were preparing the book, when the whole landscape around Hadrian's Wall turned white overnight.

The approximate location and timing of each walk were decided jointly after discussion of the landscape and vegetation of the various regions, but the exact routes were chosen only after considerable exploration of each area by the artist herself. Writer and artist joined forces for six of the walks, but the other six were undertaken separately, with the writer a few days behind the artist.

The walks we describe are mostly on well-marked footpaths and bridle-ways, with a minimum of roadwork, and they provide opportunities to explore some little-known places. Simple maps are provided for readers wishing to make the walks themselves, but the relevant Ordnance Survey maps, either 1:50,000 or 1:25,000, are strongly recommended for a fuller appreciation of the surrounding areas. The approximate length of each walk is given, but no indication of time is included because individuals walk at widely different speeds. In general, the slower you go the more you will see, and the keen naturalist will take much longer on a given walk than the enthusiastic hiker. Recommendations are given concerning footwear, especially when waterproof footwear is advisable, but this is very much a matter of personal choice. One person's walking shoes may be plimsolls or the popular 'trainers', while another walker may prefer heavy hiking boots. So 'walking shoes' can be taken to mean any reasonably practical and comfortable footwear. High heels are not recommended.

Walking can generate a healthy thirst and appetite, and suggestions are given for their satisfaction where possible. Licensing hours vary from place to place and it is a good plan to discover them before setting out.

Enjoy your walking, and please follow the Country Code.

THE COUNTRY CODE

Leave no Litter
Fasten all Gates
Avoid Damaging Fences, Hedges, and Walls
Guard against all Risk of Fire
Keep Dogs under Proper Control
Keep to the Paths across Farm Land
Safeguard Water Supplies
Protect Wildlife, Wild Plants, and Trees
Go Carefully on Country Roads
Respect the Life of the Countryside

March traditionally comes in like a lion and goes out like a lamb, and this distinct improvement in the weather is accompanied as the month unfolds by a marked increase in the number of flowers as well as a noticeable upsurge in animal activity. But early March is by no means a bad time to explore the Tywi estuary and to enjoy its remarkably verdant landscapes. Even this early in the year there is an amazing variety of greens in every bank and hedgerow. The village of Llanstephan itself appears to nestle on a dark green carpet clothing the tongue of land between the mouths of the Taf and Tywi rivers. It is tucked into the west bank of Tywi, about nine miles south-west of Carmarthen, with the remains of a Norman castle perched 200 feet above it on the cliffs to the south. These cliffs, partly clothed with trees on the landward side, stretch right round the southern tip of the peninsula. Steep grazing pastures rise up on the west of the village, while flat alluvial meadows stretch like green ribbons along the fertile valley to the north-east.

I explored Llanstephan and the area to the south of it at the beginning of March and, although I probably saw less wildlife than I would have seen later in the month, I found plenty to interest me on the cliff-tops and on the shore, and even in the village itself. I rarely moved more than a few paces without stopping to examine a new plant or animal, to listen to the birds, or simply to admire the superb views of the estuary and the surrounding landscapes.

The walk is a little over 2 miles. There is a steep climb up the steps to the cliff-top, and another tiring climb if you wish to visit the castle, but otherwise the route is quite easy apart from the heavy mud which clings to your boots along the path from Scott's Bay. Stout walking shoes or boots are recommended, although waterproof boots are better if you intend to explore the water's edge, for the shore is very muddy in places. Morning or early afternoon.

Food and drink can be obtained from The Sticks or The Castle Inn in Llanstephan.

Cars can be left in the sea front car park. Map Ref: SN353105. Unless the tide is exceptionally high, drop down to the beach and walk towards the river mouth. If the tide makes this impossible or undesirable, follow the footpath through the trees and straight up to the cliff-top path below the castle remains. You can then explore the beach at the end of your walk, when the tide has receded.

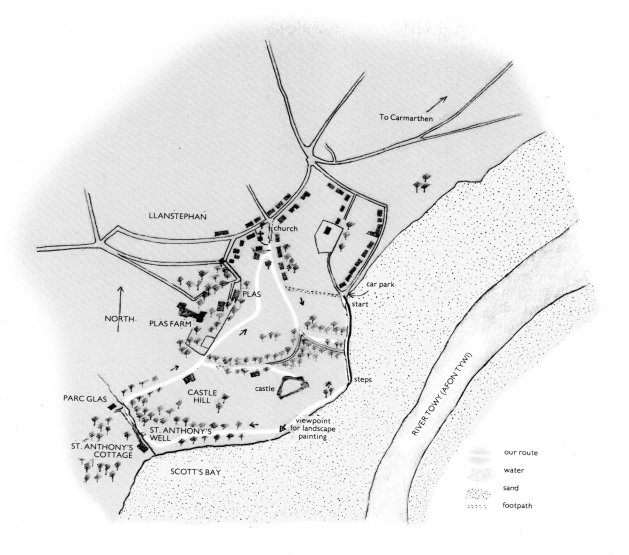

To Carmarthen

LLANSTEPHAN

church

car park

start

PLAS

NORTH

PLAS FARM

castle

steps

CASTLE
HILL

PARC GLAS

RIVER TOWY (AFON TYWI)

ST. ANTHONY'S
WELL

viewpoint
for landscape
painting

ST. ANTHONY'S
COTTAGE

SCOTT'S BAY

our route
water
sand
footpath

Overleaf: Scott's Bay at low tide, seen from the footpath just below the castle. Morning mist still lingers over the bay, but the wide expanse of sand and mud — feeding ground of thousands of oystercatchers and other waders — is clearly seen. Bracken clothes most of the steeper, uncultivated slopes, last year's golden brown fronds soon to be covered up by fresh green shoots. Numerous lichens grow close to the footpath.

*One of the several kinds of
pixie-cup lichens that grow on the steep
banks close to the cliff-top path.*

The Tywi estuary is famous for its
cockles, and the abundance of these
molluscs became obvious to me as
soon as I set foot on the beach
below the car park, for thousands
of empty shells are washed up by
each tide. The animals live two
or three centimetres below the mud
and sand, and when covered by the tide they send
up two muscular tubes called siphons. Water is
drawn in through one siphon, and microscopic food
particles are extracted from it before it is pumped out through
the other siphon. You can watch this activity very easily by digging up a cockle and
putting it in a jar of sand and sea water – but don't expect to dig up anything worth
eating on the upper part of the shore, because the cockles here are all rather small.
Large specimens nearly all come from further out in the estuary, where they are
covered by the tide most of the time and therefore have many more hours in which
to feed. Fishermen rake them from the mud at low tide. Empty razor shells are also
common on the beach, but you are unlikely to dig up living specimens because their
muscular bodies can dig into the sand faster than you can.

The land rises immediately to the south of the car park, and red cliffs towered
above me as I walked along the shore. The rocks belong to the lowest divisions of the
Old Red Sandstone and are collectively known as the Red Marls, although there are
some dull green beds among them. In texture they range from relatively soft marls
to coarse, hard sandstones. This variation was obvious as soon as I reached the cliffs,
with a fine-grained mudstone, much shattered on its exposed face, lying on top of
beds of coarser sandstones. These rocks were laid down early in the Devonian Period,
about 390 million years ago, but they experienced a good deal of uplift and folding at
the end of the succeeding Carboniferous Period and the beds are now far from level.

Close to the car park they slope, or dip, quite steeply to the north, while a little further along, where the other side of the fold is exposed, they dip to the south. The Red Marls extend throughout the Llanstephan area, but the valleys are generally floored with boulder clay brought down by the Ice Age glaciers less than a million years ago. Much of the village lies on a deposit of boulder clay.

Trees grow right to the edge of the cliffs and many of their roots are exposed where the rock has crumbled away. The shiny round leaves of navelwort sprout from nearly every crack in the upper parts of the cliffs. This plant, which is a relative of the stonecrop, is very common on rocks and walls in the damper and more westerly parts of Britain, but only where the rocks are free from lime. I was particularly attracted by the abundant grey and orange lichens clothing the rocks just above high water mark, but I had to approach them carefully because the lower rocks, which are under water at high tide, are covered with extremely slippery green seaweeds.

While examining the lichens, I was aware that I was also being watched – by some tiny grey creatures peering out from the rock crevices. I kept still, and they gradually emerged to reveal carrot-shaped bodies each with three slender 'tails' at the hind end: they were bristletails – *Petrobius maritimus* – primitive, wingless insects related to the silverfish that we get in our houses. They browse on the lichens and on debris thrown up by the waves. They are active mainly by night, but readily emerge by day in dull, damp weather. Another animal remained quite still: it was an early grey moth, beautifully camouflaged against the carpet of grey lichen. I can't say that a bird would never find the insect, but camouflage of this kind must be a very effective form of protection.

A steep flight of steps rises from the beach on the first corner, but I did not climb them right away. As the tide was receding, I walked a little further along the beach to examine some more rocks. You can, in fact, walk right round to Scott's Bay on the beach when the tide is out, but it is hard going because your feet sink into the soft sand at every step. Those rocks and boulders that lie below high water mark bear dense patches of barnacles. Looking like miniature white volcanoes, these creatures seem quite lifeless when out of water, but when the tide returns and covers them the shell plates open up and feathery limbs move rhythmically in and out to comb small food particles from the water. The barnacles are actually related to the crabs and lobsters and they float freely in the water when young. The youngsters can settle anywhere when they are ready to attach themselves to the rocks, but only those that settle in suitable places can survive. If they settle too high on the shore they risk death from desiccation or starvation, and if they settle too low down or in places that are too sheltered they are likely to find the rocks already clothed with seaweeds. The barnacles thus come to occupy a distinct zone just below high tide level, usually where they are exposed to the full force of the waves.

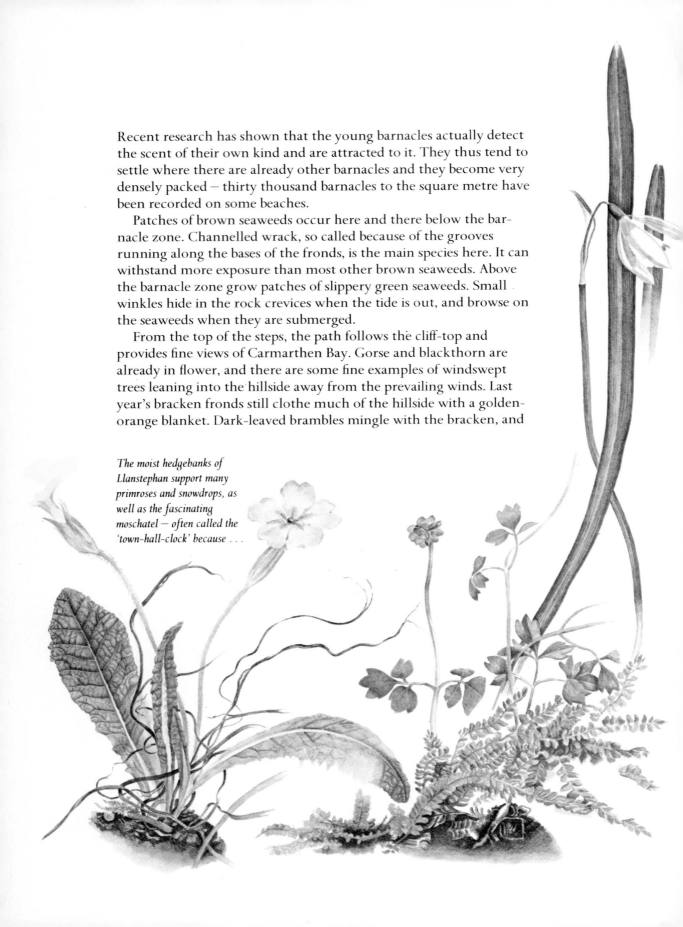

Recent research has shown that the young barnacles actually detect the scent of their own kind and are attracted to it. They thus tend to settle where there are already other barnacles and they become very densely packed – thirty thousand barnacles to the square metre have been recorded on some beaches.

Patches of brown seaweeds occur here and there below the barnacle zone. Channelled wrack, so called because of the grooves running along the bases of the fronds, is the main species here. It can withstand more exposure than most other brown seaweeds. Above the barnacle zone grow patches of slippery green seaweeds. Small winkles hide in the rock crevices when the tide is out, and browse on the seaweeds when they are submerged.

From the top of the steps, the path follows the cliff-top and provides fine views of Carmarthen Bay. Gorse and blackthorn are already in flower, and there are some fine examples of windswept trees leaning into the hillside away from the prevailing winds. Last year's bracken fronds still clothe much of the hillside with a golden-orange blanket. Dark-leaved brambles mingle with the bracken, and

The moist hedgebanks of Llanstephan support many primroses and snowdrops, as well as the fascinating moschatel — often called the 'town-hall-clock' because ...

wrens scamper through them in search of
food. I heard the wrens' loud, piping calls once or
twice, but for much of the time they were drowned by the chorus
of curlews and oystercatchers on the muddy shore below.

Oystercatchers are attractive black and white birds, easily identified
by their long, red bills. Their calls include a short,
shrill *pic-pic-pic* as well as the more familiar and
penetrating *cleep-cleep-cleep.* Cocklecatchers might be
a better name for them, for they rarely feed on
oysters, and cockles are certainly their main
food in this area. They are shovelled up from the
mud and quickly hammered open with the beak. When
the valves are partly open in shallow water, the oystercatcher
cleverly inserts the tip of its beak and levers the shell open even
more. The closure muscles are torn, and the shell then gapes
open for the bird to remove the flesh. The shores of Carmarthen
Bay, and especially those of the Burry Inlet to the east, are
favourite wintering grounds for oystercatchers, some of which
come from as far away as Iceland and Norway. They are sometimes
accused of damaging the cockle industry, but the cockles are so
abundant that even large flocks probably have little effect on the
population. Crabs and worms also contribute to the oystercatcher's
diet, and large numbers of mussels are eaten in some places.

*. . . each head has four faces like a clock tower. Each face
is composed of one flower, and there is a fifth flower
carried horizontally on the top. Hazel catkins in the
hedges have already scattered most of their pollen.*

The edges of the cliff path below the bracken support extensive patches of pixie-cup lichens, whose miniature goblets spring up from carpets of greyish-green scales. It had rained heavily before my walk, and when I saw them many of the goblets held glistening globules of water. Rain drops falling into the goblets help to scatter the minute flakes that grow into new lichen plants. Before dropping down to Scott's Bay, the path goes through a thinly wooded area, and here I made my first real contact with the riot of greenery that was to remain with me for the rest of my walk. The greens ranged from the pale yellowish variety of the mosses around the tree trunks to the dark, shiny greens of the lords-and-ladies leaves, and the bright yellow flowers of the lesser celandine shone star-like against this green carpet. I also found flowers of red campion, whose long, straggling stems suggested that they had been flowering throughout the winter. Hart's tongue fern, hard to recognize as a fern until you have seen the rows of spore capsules under the tongue-like fronds, grows particularly well here, in company with several more typical fern species.

At Scott's Bay – named after a Captain Scott who built the cottage standing at the head of the bay – I had another chance to see the red and green sandstones. If the tide allows, you can walk a little further along the beach to Wharley Point, where the rock layers have been tilted into an almost vertical position; but do not attempt this walk when the tide is coming in! From Scott's Bay, the route turns inland along the muddy track to the right of the cottage. St Anthony's Well, a short distance up on the left, is dedicated to the Roman Saint Anthony, although no one seems to know why. A figure of the saint is said to have stood in a niche above the water at one time. According to some writers, the water once possessed healing powers, but it now seems to have lost its efficacy and no cures are actually documented. Other people believe that the well was just a wishing well for the lovelorn. Regardless of its history, the damp stonework provides an ideal site for mosses. Several species grow here, and on close examination I saw that they were being grazed by numerous small snails with reddish-brown or purple, spindle-shaped shells. I noticed a strong smell of garlic in this area, coming from the bright green leaves of wild garlic, or ramsons, springing up along the path. By the end of the month they will probably be accompanied by heads of star-like white flowers. I also saw wild snowdrops flowering under the trees.

The track from the beach had so far been mainly on the boulder clay, which explained its stickiness, but I soon turned right into a wider track and rose up on to the Red Marls again. However there is no obvious difference in the flora here because the boulder clay is derived largely from the marls. The track is a sunken lane, with primroses in flower and an abundance of ferns on the steep banks. The fronds are still green, but most of them are limp and past their best. Apart from the hart's tongue fern, most of the ferns look alike at first glance, but a closer look at the fronds shows that there are several different species, each with its own characteristic pattern of frond division. New fronds, clothed with protective brown scales, are waiting, still tightly coiled, at the base of each plant. Ferns revel in the humid atmosphere of the sunken lanes because this provides the moisture so vital to their rather complex reproductive processes. The softly hairy leaves and shoots of creeping soft grass contrast strongly with the brighter greens of the ferns, and many other flowering plants add to the fantastic mosaic of greens on the banks. The pale blue flowers of the germander speedwell, or bird's-eye, peer out from the hedges, and around the farm gates they are joined by the flowers of the common field speedwell, which are borne singly instead of in spikes.

Although March was still most definitely in lionly mood, I climbed up to Llanstephan Castle ruins and was well rewarded with a splendid view across the Tywi to Ferryside. It was low tide, and fishermen in a small boat were busy with their nets in mid-channel, hoping to trap the mature, firm-fleshed salmon that are coming back to the river at this time of year. Even if the fish have been away at sea for several years, a wonderful chemical sense ensures that they return to the very river in which they were born. Incidentally, further up the Tywi you can still see men fishing from traditional coracles.

A kestrel enjoys a meal of carrion snatched from the strand line. Opposite: a buzzard.

The castle was built early in the twelfth century, but the oldest remaining parts
date from the thirteenth century. The walls are of hard sandstone, and form
a most attractive background for the navelwort and other plants that grow in the
crevices. I was fascinated by the numerous ferns growing in the well shaft. Ferns
can spring up in the most obscure places because their
spores are so tiny and are blown everywhere. Those that
land in suitably damp places – and the well walls certainly
fit this requirement – eventually produce new ferns.

*Sweet violets and
the fascinating hart's-
tongue fern grow under
the spindly elms
fringing the cliff-
top path.*

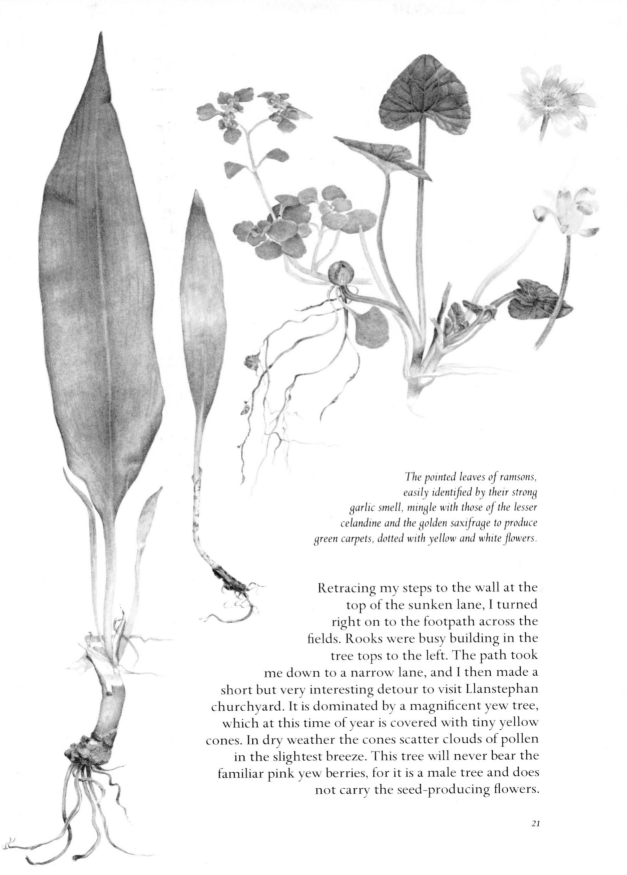

*The pointed leaves of ramsons,
easily identified by their strong
garlic smell, mingle with those of the lesser
celandine and the golden saxifrage to produce
green carpets, dotted with yellow and white flowers.*

Retracing my steps to the wall at the top of the sunken lane, I turned right on to the footpath across the fields. Rooks were busy building in the tree tops to the left. The path took me down to a narrow lane, and I then made a short but very interesting detour to visit Llanstephan churchyard. It is dominated by a magnificent yew tree, which at this time of year is covered with tiny yellow cones. In dry weather the cones scatter clouds of pollen in the slightest breeze. This tree will never bear the familiar pink yew berries, for it is a male tree and does not carry the seed-producing flowers.

21

The shiny round leaves of navelwort spring from every stonewall as well as from crevices in the cliffs. The leaves provide food and shelter for many small animals, including the garden snail seen here. The little door snail at the top of the picture is also very common on old walls, coming out from the crevices at night or in damp weather to browse on algae and mosses.

Several tall and straggly Japanese red cedars also grow in the churchyard, their normally bright green foliage still tinged with the reddish colour which it assumes for the winter. Although these trees look quite ancient, they are unlikely to be antiques, for the species was not introduced to Britain until 1861. Ivy, now carrying juicy black fruits, sprawls over the walls and gravestones. Many of the stones also bear conspicuous patches of lichen. These grow very slowly, and at a more or less constant rate in a given situation. The dates on the stones give you an approximate

22

age for the lichens, and if you measure the diameter of a few patches you can get some idea of the growth rate. Many encrusting species increase their diameters by between one and two millimetres each year.

Entering the lane again and turning right, I was fascinated by the abundance of plant life on the stone walls, and soon reaching for my field guide to check identifications. The glossy, rounded and partly dissected leaves of the shining cranesbill mingle with the equally shiny leaves of the ivy-leaved toadflax and the ubiquitous navelwort, and scattered plants of herb robert give promise of rich colour later in the year. Further along, past the dark Monterey pines on the left, I found wall rue, maidenhair spleenwort, and rusty-back ferns peering out from the wall. Although these wall-loving ferns do grow in the eastern parts of Britain, they are much more common in the damper climate of the west. Llanstephan has only a moderate rainfall of about 39 inches each year, but the seaside location ensures that the humidity is plenty high enough for the ferns' reproductive processes. The walls also support dense patches of stonecrop on their tops, together with common field speedwell and the tiny-flowered wall speedwell. The most striking thing about these walls, however, is the blanket of pale grey lichen that coats almost every stone and makes it look like limestone. The lichen is called *Ochrolechia parella*, and it is the same species as the grey one that harboured the bristletails down by the shore. Each patch has a white border and little pinkish brown blobs near the centre. These blobs, which look like tiny treacle tarts under a lens, are the spore-bearing bodies. Many of the lichen patches have run together, but if you can find a fairly distinct patch you can measure its diameter. Comparison with the churchyard lichens will give some idea of the minimum age of the wall. Interesting as the wall flora may be, don't forget to look up from time to time: you may well see buzzards circling above the castle or gliding over the pastures in their search for food.

A footpath leaves the lane close to the Monterey pines and runs down to the car park, but I was too engrossed with the wall plants and I continued to the end of the lane and turned down the fern-fringed lane to the beach. Drifts of opposite-leaved golden saxifrage made my additional walk worth while, and a flock of jackdaws scavenging along the strand-line greeted my return to the beach. The birds perched hopefully on the sea wall as I ate an apple in the car, and they made short work of the core. Next time, I must take something more exciting for them.

Spring
APRIL
Helford and Gillan Creek, Cornwall

S pring comes early to the Cornish countryside – our florists get most of their early tulips and daffodils from here – and by April the lanes and hedgerows are ablaze with colourful wild flowers set against a background of innumerable greens. Many narcissi which have escaped from cultivation now perch daintily on the roadside banks. You can enjoy the Cornish lanes and footpaths and their wildlife to the full at this time of year because, although spring comes early, the tourists do not: I met just twelve people on my walk.

The walk is based on the secluded village of Helford, and takes in a fascinating mixture of inland and marine features. Sheltered, wooded valleys alternate with grazing meadows and bulb fields, but the most spectacular features are the numerous tidal creeks, which are really the drowned lower reaches of river valleys. A rise in sea level since the ice ages, combined with a slight sinking of the land in this area, allowed the sea to invade considerable stretches of the rivers, forming the branching estuaries so characteristic of the region and so much loved by yachtsmen. High tides reach far up the tributary valleys, but when the tides recede you can see the streams which once babbled through rich woodland meandering forlornly across the extensive mud-flats. In several parts of the West Country you can even see submerged forests exposed at low tide.

I knew it was going to be a good walk before I even got out of my car. The sun was shining, the lanes leading to Helford were bright with spring flowers, and within seconds of my switching off the engine a robin had swooped down to perch on my wing mirror. I didn't know whether he was welcoming me, warning me that I was trespassing on his territory, or merely being inquisitive, but he was certainly not afraid of me. He quickly summoned his wife when I threw out some broken biscuits and each time she opened her beak he obligingly popped in some crumbs. She was probably incubating some eggs in a nest nearby, for she did not stay long.

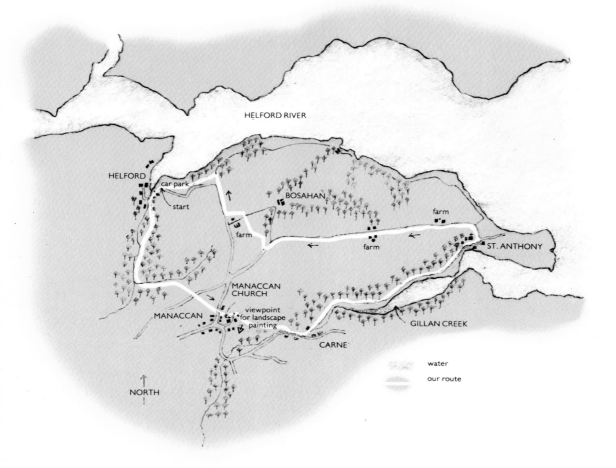

HELFORD RIVER

HELFORD

car park

start

BOSAHAN

farm

farm

farm

farm

ST. ANTHONY

MANACCAN
CHURCH

viewpoint
for landscape
painting

MANACCAN

GILLAN CREEK

CARNE

water

our route

↑
NORTH

The walk is about 5 miles long and fairly hilly, although the hills are not too steep and the walking is not difficult. The woodland paths can be muddy after rain, but normal walking shoes should be sufficient.

The walk is best started in the morning. An excellent pub lunch, washed down with equally excellent beer, can be obtained at the New Inn in Manaccan.

Cars must be left in the Helford car park just above the village. Map Ref: SW 759260.

Overleaf: Looking south up the tree-lined valley from the footpath near Manaccan. The stream swings to the left in the centre of the picture, on its way down to Gillan Creek. Mist hangs in the valley, but the distinctive pink of the bursting sycamore buds and their young leaves shines through as though the trees were bathed in red light.

But the male continued to feed even when I got out of the car and sat on the grass with him. We were soon joined by a cock blackbird and six pairs of chaffinches. This was something of a surprise, for chaffinches are usually strongly territorial in the breeding season and the males are generally agressive towards each other. I suspect that the birds' nests were well spread out, but that the car park yielded so many picnic scraps that the birds treated it as a communal feeding ground. All were very tame, and in another part of the car park — probably nearer to their own nests — chaffinches were also perching on the cars and demanding to be fed.

I eventually tore myself away from the car park and walked out into the main street of Helford — a street just wide enough for a car to pass you without running over your toes. Chusan palms flourish in several gardens and testify to the mildness of the Cornish climate, while hundreds of ivy-leaved toadflax flowers peer from the stone walls like so many little goofy faces. The footpath to Manaccan leaves Helford by way of a narrow, wooded valley with a steep bank rising up on the left. The trees, many of them densely clothed with lichens, include oaks, beeches, elms, ashes, and sycamores. The leaves of the latter were already well developed when I was there, but

the path was still only partly shaded and the banks carried a wealth of spring flowers.

Primroses, violets and lesser celandines were particularly abundant, scattered bluebells and red campions were already in flower, and the white flowers of the ramsons — wild garlic — were beginning to spill from their sheaths. The smell from their leaves vied with that of the primroses.

Primroses and celandines apart, the most conspicuous plants to my eyes were the ferns — mainly the hart's tongue fern and the prickly shield fern. The old fronds were still dark green and many remained upright, but it was the new fronds that caught my attention. Those of the hart's tongue were pale green, tightly clustered, and partly unfurled, looking like those noisy toy 'snakes' that children love to blow in your face. The fronds of the prickly shield fern are much larger. Densely clothed with brown scales, the partly unrolled fronds lean backwards; they remind me of cobras rearing up and spreading their hoods ready to strike. Mosses and liverworts clothe the steep banks beneath the ferns. Bird song accompanied me as I walked up the valley: tits and nuthatches piped in the tree tops, and chaffinches called vigorously from the lower branches.

The chaffinches of Helford car park were amazingly tame, the males perching on the cars and striking a variety of intriguing poses. The less brightly coloured females (bottom left) were a little less bold, but still gathered around the cars to wait for food. Robins behaved in a similar way in another part of the car park, but only one pair in a given place.

Blackbirds, wrens, and song thrushes added to the chorus, which was regularly punctuated by the harsh, rasping calls of some golden pheasants introduced to the area a few years ago. The shells of hazel-nuts neatly split in half indicated the presence of squirrels: red squirrels are known in the area, but I only saw some grey ones. The strong smell of a fox lingered here and there along the damp path, and well-marked tracks showed where he regularly crossed the path on his nightly patrols. But the dominant smell was that of the primroses. A small stream runs close to the path, and the slope between path and stream was covered with drifts of these beautiful flowers, although close to the water the primrose yellow gave way to the darker yellow of the opposite-leaved golden saxifrage.

mosses

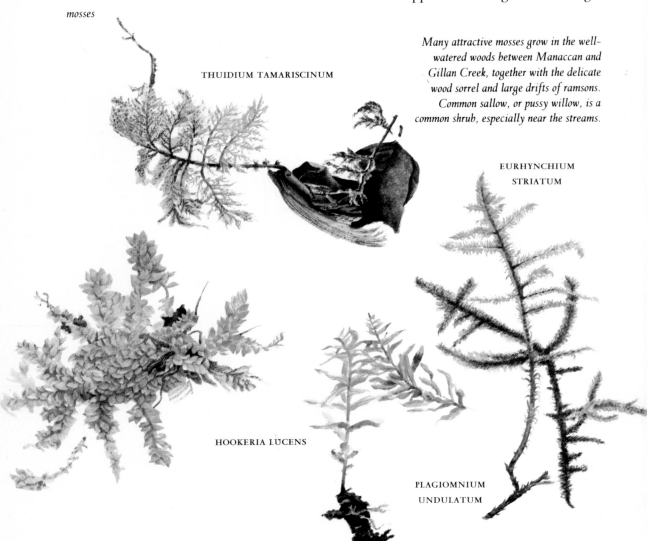

THUIDIUM TAMARISCINUM

Many attractive mosses grow in the well-watered woods between Manaccan and Gillan Creek, together with the delicate wood sorrel and large drifts of ramsons. Common sallow, or pussy willow, is a common shrub, especially near the streams.

EURHYNCHIUM
STRIATUM

HOOKERIA LUCENS

PLAGIOMNIUM
UNDULATUM

common sallow

POLYTRICHUM
COMMUNE

ramsons or wild garlic

wood sorrel

*Grey squirrels love to play hide-and-seek
wth walkers, often sitting on the ground with
eyes twinkling as if to say 'Come on,
catch me if you can': of course, we can't.*

There is something magnetic
about a rippling stream, and
I found the attraction irresistible.
It was an exciting detour, for I had been
sitting by the water for only a few minutes
when a bundle of brown fur rushed along the opposite bank.
It was a water vole and it was being pursued by another brown
object. This second creature was slimmer than the first and the black
tip to its tail identified it as a stoat. Both animals were quickly lost
to view, but I heard no screams and assumed that the vole had escaped.

Returning to the path, I carried on up the valley, still surrounded by rich flora.
The effect of the sunshine was very marked in some of the clearings, where the
flowers were much further advanced. Greater stitchwort – 'shirt-buttons' I learned
to call it as a small boy – became prominent and remained with me for much of the
rest of my walk. Towards the head of the valley, I came to the first of several stiles
built in typical Cornish fashion with slabs of stone set in small walls. The slabs are
often, but not always, of granite and are clearly much more durable than the more
usual wooden stiles. Beyond the stile, I found myself in a beautiful sunken lane
whose banks were yellow with primroses.

A large sallow tree that had been blown down had formed a bridge about two
metres above the path. Squirrels clearly used it as a dining table, judging by the
numerous hazel-nut shells around it, and a pile of feathers about halfway across
suggested that the tree also served as a plucking post for a sparrowhawk. These birds
of prey capture most of their victims in mid-air and then carry them to a convenient
perch where they remove much of the plumage before eating the flesh.

Another dead tree was covered with the aptly-named King Alfred's Cakes – hard,
black, hemispherical outgrowths that look just like burnt buns. They are, in fact, the
fruiting bodies of a fungus that grows in the dead wood. They are sometimes known
as 'cramp balls' because they were once thought to ward off cramp if carried about.
But don't be tempted to break one off and put it in your pocket, for millions of black
spores are fired off from the surface and they surround the fungus with a soot-like
deposit.

— move towards them and they are off up the nearest
tree, peering mischievously at us first from one side of
the trunk and then from the other. Bulbs, buds, and
tender shoots are the squirrels' main food in
spring, but watch patiently and you may see one
suddenly start to dig frantically and unearth
a buried hazel nut. The shell is then neatly nipped
in half and discarded, while the kernel is eaten
with obvious pleasure.

The path emerges from the trees at the head of the valley and crosses rich grazing meadows. I was aware of some bright red splashes away to my left and realized that here was one of the bulb fields. Had I been a few days earlier, I would have seen the flower-gathering in full swing, but the only colour now lay in the heaps of discarded flowers – blemished and distorted ones, and precocious individuals that had opened early and would not then fit into the neat bunches required for market.

A good crop of stinging nettles was growing along the hedgerows. The nettle tops are good to eat at this time of year and make an excellent substitute for spinach. Several kinds of caterpillars also enjoy stinging nettles, and already a small tortoiseshell butterfly was examining the plants in readiness for laying her eggs. Lesser celandines were abundant along this south-facing bank, and I discovered quite a variation in their deep yellow flowers. The normal complement of petals is eight, but I found flowers with six, seven, nine, and even eleven petals. Violets were also plentiful along the hedgebank, and furry brown carder bees were busy collecting nectar from them. These bumble bees normally nest on the surface of the ground and would have found the south-facing hedgebank much to their liking. Most other bumble bees nest under the ground, often in old mouse holes.

My route took me through the village of Manaccan and then, keeping the church on my right, into another footpath leading to Carne. Numerous seven-spot ladybirds were sunning themselves on the shiny navelwort leaves, and no doubt growing fat on the abundant blackfly infesting the red campion. The blackfly were probably also feeding the brood of a pair of long-tailed tits which spluttered excitedly as I passed through their territory.

The path led me into another wooded valley full of flowers. The bluebells were well out in this sun-trap, and the dandelions by the path had already produced their fluffy seed-heads. Blackthorn petals were falling like confetti on to the ferns and ramsons below. Polypodies and other ferns grow high in the trees in the lower, damper parts of this delightful valley.

A holly hedge grows close to where the path meets the road, and if you look at the leaves you will see that a very high proportion have a pale blotch near the centre. Each blotch, which is technically known as a leaf mine, is the work of the grub of a tiny fly. The grub feeds on the tissues between the upper and lower surface of the leaf, and the removal of the tissues produces the pale blotch. At this time of year, most of the grubs have turned into pale brown pupae, which you can find by gently opening the leaves.

The next section of the walk is along the road to St Anthony, but this is no ordinary road. It is a narrow track along the edge of Gillan Creek, and there are new discoveries to be made at every turn. It was low tide when I arrived, and the stream which had been rippling through the woodland a mere 200 yards back up the road was now a muddy trickle flowing through mud flats and seaweeds. It was strange to see and smell

The liverwort LUNULARIA CRUCIATA, *recognized by its crescent-shaped gemma cups containing detachable buds (gemmae), was found growing on the banks of the stream just above Gillan Creek.*

these seaweeds and not see the sea, but the open water was beyond the tall Monterey pines standing majestically over a bend in the creek. The banks of the creek support an assortment of trees, which are densely clothed with grey lichens. The most conspicuous of these are the beard lichens of the genus *Usnea*, which sprout from the branches like tufts of tangled hair. The somewhat coarser *Ramalina calicaris* also forms numerous tufts, studded with pale, spore-producing discs, while other more leaf-like species completely conceal the bark on the upper surfaces of the branches.

Several blackthorn trees grow by the roadside, and I spent some minutes watching a white-tailed bumble bee busy among the blossoms. She was so engrossed in her work that I was able to stroke her at will. She seemed to be collecting nectar only, for her pollen baskets were quite empty and she made no attempt to brush pollen from her body while I watched, but there were plenty of other bumble bees around that were collecting pollen. They can transport up to sixty per cent of their own weight in pollen, ramming it into the 'baskets' on their hind legs until it forms two bulging yellow masses. At this time of year the bees are all queens: they have only recently woken from hibernation and are now busy rearing their first broods.

Woolly bears are common on low-growing plants in spring and were seen at several points on the walk. They are the caterpillars of the garden tiger moth.

red campion

germander speedwell

bugle

common
field speedwell

common
dog violet

Flowers are everywhere in Cornwall in April. The earliest ones are mostly white or yellow, but other colours appear in profusion towards the end of the month, when the red campion makes a welcome splash on the white and green carpet of stitchwort on the hedgebanks. Drifts of blue germander speedwell complete the patriotic patchwork. Bugle, lesser periwinkle, and wild strawberry were just some of the other flowers in evidence on the banks above Gillan Creek, while the common dog violet peered shyly from nearly every yard of the walk. Small tortoiseshell butterflies — one of the earliest species to wake from their winter slumbers — alternately sunbathed and sought nectar from the flowers.

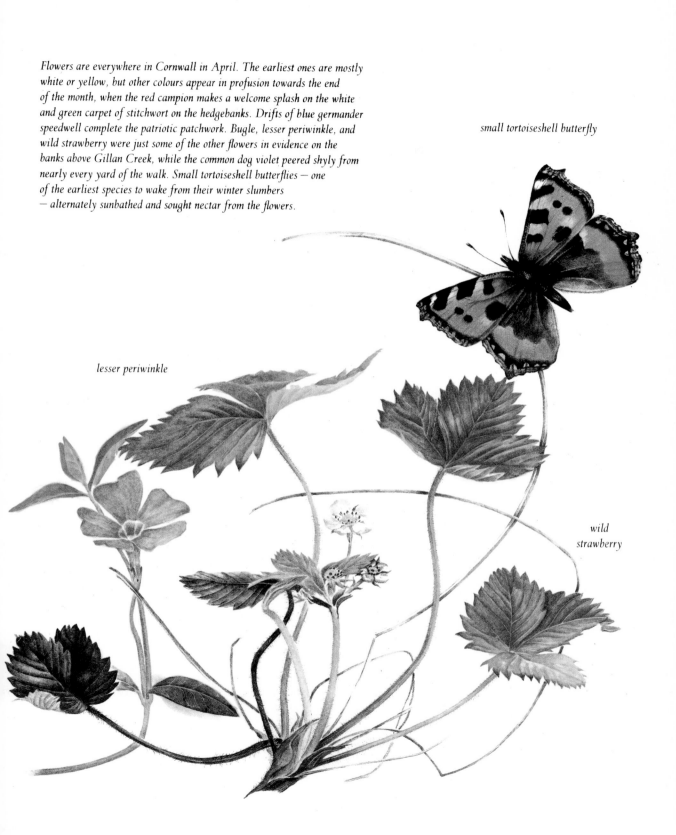

small tortoiseshell butterfly

lesser periwinkle

wild strawberry

I could see that the abundant primroses were being visited by several kinds of bees and also by many drone-flies – hover-flies which bear a remarkable similarity to honey bees, but dart away much more readily than bees when you approach them. Dozens of them hovered overhead. As well as collecting pollen and nectar from the primroses, these insects perform the all-important function of pollination, without which the flowers cannot set seed. Look carefully at the throats of a number of primroses and you will see that there are two different types. One, known as pin-eyed, has the stigma at the entrance to the throat and the stamens further down; the other type, known as thrum-eyed, has the stamens at the top and the stigma further down. This arrangement encourages cross-pollination, or out-breeding, for a bee collecting pollen high up on its tongue from a thrum-eyed flower is most likely to rub some off on the stigma of a pin-eyed flower – which would grow on a different plant.

Helford's muddy creek may not be inviting to human eyes, but it is heaven for various water birds. I saw several herons standing in the shallow water or walking about in the hope of stirring up some tasty morsels, while a pair of shelducks and two swans swam lazily upstream. Scores of gulls squawked noisily on the mud, and grey wagtails skimmed over the surface to snatch up midges and other small insects.

As the road rose high above the creek, I was aware of a new smell replacing that of the seaweeds and primroses: like that of a fox, and yet slightly different. I was in badger country. Tracks through the undergrowth, together with extensive diggings among the bluebells, confirmed the existence of these beautiful animals, and I had visions of them sleeping soundly beneath me as I walked along. A young rabbit peered cautiously from the hedge: he was relatively safe in the middle of the day, but he would have to be careful when brock woke in the evening.

A pair of jackdaws greeted me as I passed the Church of St Anthony, and looking up I saw that *Ramalina* lichens were even growing high on the tower. The white flowers of the three-cornered leek – so called because of its triangular stem – sprang up from the gateway. This relative of the ramsons was introduced from the Mediterranean region and is now common in many Cornish lanes. The church itself could also be described as foreign, for it is built of a fine-grained granite from Normandy. It dates from the twelfth century, and according to legend it was built by a group of grateful Normans who managed to get ashore at St Anthony after a shipwreck.

A cliff-fall prevented me from completing my walk by way of the cliff-top path, and I had to return to Helford mainly by road, but it was a colourful journey with red campion and stitchwort covering large areas of the hedgebank with a red and white patchwork. A peacock butterfly was enjoying the sunshine after its long hibernation. It would have flown for a couple of months or more during the previous summer and was now rather tattered, contrasting strongly with the pristine appearance of the orange-tips which had only just left their pupae.

I watched the bumble bees again and noticed a stranger in their midst. It was slightly less hairy than the others and had darker wings. It was a cuckoo bee — a type of bumble bee that does not make its own nest. The female waits for the other bumble bees to establish their nests and rear a few workers, and then she invades one of the nests and lays her eggs in it. The cuckoo bees have no workers, and the workers of the host species rear the young cuckoo bees.

The path for Helford leaves the lane just after you pass a clump of tall Monterey pines, but be careful as you walk under these trees. Rooks build here, and a tree-top scuffle dislodged a large old cone which only narrowly missed my head. Look far to the west just before you turn into the footpath and you will see the giant dish-like aerials of Goonhilly Downs, where television pictures and telephone conversations are gathered in from satellites high above the Atlantic. Immense strides have been made in communications since Marconi sent his first radio signals across the Atlantic from Cornwall in 1901, but some things have not changed: the tide was still out when I returned to Helford, and men were out there raking cockles from the mud just as they have been doing for centuries.

Spring
MAY
The Cerne Valley, Dorset

I f anything in our geologically diverse countryside can be said to typify English scenery it is the chalk downland. This is one of the most distinctive types of scenery, and it covers a large part of southern England. One of its characteristics is the smoothness of its contours, resulting from the relatively soft nature and porosity of the chalk rock. Rain falling on to the chalk can seep in all over the surface and, being slightly acidic, can gradually dissolve the surface layers. This process has been going on for millions of years and has produced the beautifully rounded chalk hills that we see today – a very 'comfortable' type of scenery which I personally find more relaxing than any other. The rolling downs are like giant armchairs, upholstered with a cloth of green grass. The seats of the 'chairs' are the numerous smooth-sided valleys that dissect the downs, cut by streams that flowed during wetter periods just before and just after the ice ages. Now the water table is way below the floors of most of these valleys and they are dry. The porous chalk acts like a gigantic sponge and soaks up vast quantities of water. In a really wet winter, the level may rise above the floors of some of the lower valleys, and then streams known as bournes or winterbournes start to flow; but they survive only while the water table is high. Most streams in downland flow along the bottoms of the steeper slopes, where they are fed by water issuing from springs.

All of these downland features can be seen in Dorset around the village of Cerne Abbas, which is near the western edge of the chalk outcrop. The area also has a good deal of natural history interest and, in common with many other chalk areas, it has a long human history. Being light and well drained, the chalklands were among the first areas to be settled and traversed by roads, and we find many historic sites on the downland. Dorset has its fair share, among which the Cerne Giant, cut into the

The walk is about 6½ miles, with a long, although not particularly steep, climb near the beginning. The ground is rough in places, and there is a second, shorter climb beyond half-way. Normal walking shoes are suitable, but these should have plenty of grip because the turf can be surprisingly slippery.

This is definitely a picnic walk, to be started in the morning. There are many fine places to sit and enjoy the scenery with your food, and Cerne Abbas can offer teashops on your return in the afternoon.

Cars may be parked in Abbey Street close to the churchyard. Map Ref. ST 666013.

Overleaf: Looking west from Farm Hill to the lower and more gentle slopes of the chalk, extensively cultivated and now supporting wheat in full growth after the spring rains. In a couple of months this scene will be golden yellow and ready for the combine harvester.

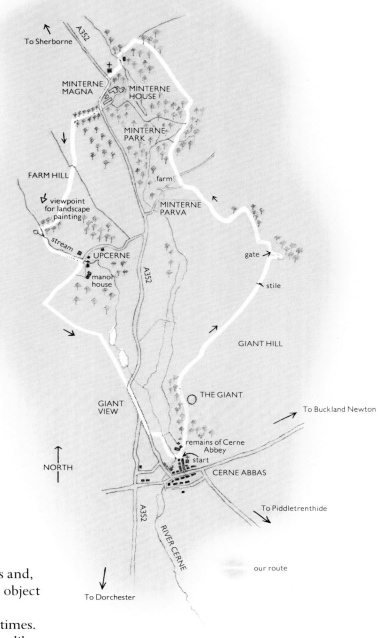

turf above Cerne Abbas, is the most striking. He has watched over the rolling hills to the west for some eighteen centuries and, although there are people now who object to his nakedness, there can be no doubting his importance in Roman times. Geographer, naturalist and historian alike will thus find plenty to interest them in Dorset's chalk hills.

Leaving my car under the watchful eyes of a group of Muscovy ducks, I wandered into a churchyard alive with bird song. Above the chatter of the tits and warblers a cuckoo invited me to play hide-and-seek, but I could not find him in spite of his frequent 'cuckoo' and I struck out across the meadow behind the churchyard. Immense beeches towered above me as I entered the meadow, and the male catkins, now brown and dry, were falling thickly to the ground. But they had done their job and spiky cups were already swelling around the developing nuts: the grey squirrel watching me from a high branch would not go hungry in the autumn.

A cock yellowhammer perched on the fence and welcomed me to the downland with his attractive song, popularly translated as 'a little bit of bread and no cheese'. His mate, less brightly coloured, foraged in the turf nearby. Above the fence on the right stands the Cerne Giant. Only the soles of his feet can be seen from this point and, looking up the steep slope, you can appreciate the enormity of the task facing the artists who carved him in the turf. You need to be much further away to take in the whole of the 200-foot high figure, the best views being from the road towards the end of the walk.

Cattle and rabbits graze the lower slopes of Giant Hill — heavily enough to prevent much scrub encroachment, but lightly enough to allow a wide range of herbaceous plants to flower. The slopes are thus clothed with typical chalk pasture, studded with buttercups at this time of year. One of the commonest plants on the hill is the glaucous sedge, but most people probably fail to notice it as they walk over it, and those who do probably dismiss it as 'grass'. But a closer look at its bluish-green leaves and shoots will reveal the distinctly triangular arrangement so characteristic of the sedges. The flowering spikes are well developed in May. The male flowers, identified by their hanging stamens, are borne on the upper spikes, while the female flowers develop on the lower spikes.

Among the several species of grasses beginning to throw up their flowering heads during my visit were crested dog's-tail, quaking grass or totters, hairy oat, meadow oat, cocks-foot, and the very fine-leaved red fescue and sheep's fescue grasses. If you look at the bristle-like leaves of these last two grasses with a lens you will see that each blade is actually rolled round to form a cyclinder, with the breathing pores on the inside to cut down the rate of evaporation. The chalk drains very rapidly and the soil is therefore rather dry, so most of the downland plants have some method of coping with water shortage. Many have small leaves, often with hairy coatings, to cut down the rate of evaporation, while others have very long roots which reach down to the damper zones of the chalk. The salad burnet, for example, regularly sends its roots two feet into the ground. This plant is abundant on Giant Hill and its globular flower heads can be seen from June onwards. Its deeply-divided, greyish-green leaves have a slight cucumber flavour and will make an interesting filling or garnish for your mid-day sandwiches.

In common with many other chalk pasture plants, the salad burnet forms a rosette of leaves at ground level. As well as keeping the leaves out of the drying winds, this habit enables the plants to withstand trampling and reduces grazing damage to a minimum. Among the common rosette-forming plants that I saw on my walk were cowslips, dandelions, daisies, plantains, hawkbits, and, of course, the stemless thistle which can make finding a comfortable picnic spot quite difficult on some parts of the downs. The cowslips were in flower, and there were plenty of daisy and dandelion heads, but the other rosette plants were still some weeks away from opening their blooms.

We spotted a none-too-well concealed blackbird's nest in a bush near the churchyard. The hen was sitting, but then flew off to reveal three speckled eggs. She quickly returned when we had passed.

The track took me diagonally up the hillside, and as the sun began to warm the slopes the butterflies came out: meadow browns, small heaths, and wall browns were all sunning themselves on the short turf. Their prominent eye-spots serve as decoys, leading birds away from the head and towards the less vulnerable wing-tips. It is not uncommon to find these brown butterflies with beak marks around the eye-spots. The aptly-named dingy-skipper – a very moth-like butterfly – darted about close to the ground, and then I was treated to the courtship display of its cousin the grizzled skipper. This small butterfly is not very exciting at first sight, but if you can get close to it you will appreciate the beauty of its velvety black wings studded with white spots. The female sat on a cowslip leaf, seductively fluttering her wings every now and then as a girl might flutter her eyelashes. The male danced excitedly around her, settling every few seconds and vibrating his wings rapidly to waft his scent in her direction. This went on for some minutes, and he then settled facing her on the same leaf. Excitement was building, but it all came to nothing: whether my peeping-tom presence upset them, or whether they merely didn't fancy each other after all, I shall never know, but the male suddenly took off and disappeared up the slope. The female waited a few seconds and then flew down the hill. I like to think that they may have met again after I left.

Rabbits roam all over the hillsides, and where they have been scratching you can see that the soil is very shallow – rarely more than an inch or two before you reach solid chalk. The chalk itself is a very pure form of limestone, and there is little impurity left to form the soil skeleton as rain water gradually dissolves the upper layers. Soil formation on the steeper slopes is counteracted by soil-creep – the gradual downward movement of soil particles under the influence of gravity – and so the soil can never become very deep. This characteristically shallow soil of the chalk slopes is called a rendzina. Deeper soils can develop on the flatter tops of the hills: they often contain large flints, left behind when the chalk dissolved away.

The deeper soils on the top of Giant Hill, combined with reduced grazing press-ure, have allowed gorse scrub to develop, together with a good deal of blackthorn and hawthorn. The latter was in full flower at the time of my walk and the air was filled with its sweet and rather sickly scent – a great attraction for flies. A rotund black beetle stumbled through the grass, and as I picked it up it lived up to its name of 'bloody-nosed beetle' by exuding a bright red fluid from its mouth. Contrasting strongly with the beetle's black coat, this fluid, which really is blood, acts as a warn-ing to birds or other predators who might interfere with the insect.

As I was putting the beetle down again, I disturbed a green hairstreak butterfly, whose green undersides make it extremely difficult to follow in flight: its brown upper sides are exposed for a fraction of a second, and then the insect 'disappears' as the green undersides merge with the background, only for the brown to flash again a few metres further on.

At the summit of the hill the path crosses a stile and takes you round the edge of a field which seems to consist of nothing but flints — the chalk long since dissolved from the plateau was clearly one of those layers extremely rich in flint. I marvelled at how such a field could be ploughed, and even more at how such a healthy-looking cereal crop could spring from this stony ground, Judging by the number of skylarks singing above me, the birds do not mind the stones, and the builders of Cerne Abbas and neighbouring villages have certainly been glad of them, for many fine flint houses can be seen in the vicinity.

Turning up at the corner of the field, the path leads to a clump of trees underlain by a carpet of bluebells and red campion. Here I was enveloped in a cloud of black flies drifting lazily through the air and settling all over the vegetation. These were St Mark's flies, so named because they often make their first appearance around St Mark's Day (April 25th). Despite their hairy and rather sinister appearance, the flies are quite harmless, although their grubs cause considerable damage to the roots of cereals and other crops.

Brushing the flies from my hair, I turned left at the trees and immediately left again down the side of the next field to where a stile leads back on to the grazed hillside — a fine spot for a rest and a sandwich and for views of the Cerne Valley. Rolling hills stretch into the distance, while the turrets of Minterne House, the seat of Lord Digby, poke up through the trees in the valley bottom. The house was built in the eighteenth century and extended on several occasions during the nineteenth century. The additions detracted from the original appearance, however, and the house was finally rebuilt to a design by Leonard Stokes between 1902 and 1907. The superb gardens, laid out in the eighteenth century, contain some fine rhodo-dendrons. As I approached Minterne Parva, I was able to watch the silage harvest in full swing. The forage harvester moved relentlessly up and down the meadow, spewing the cut grass into trailers for transport to the silage pit: extremely efficient, but it can never have the appeal of traditional hay-making.

A herd of friendly Friesians investigated me and my ruc-sac very closely for several minutes, but concluded that I was inedible and munched their way further along the slope into the shade of some oak trees. Cow-pats are not everyone's cup of tea, but I must confess to finding them interesting from an entomological point of view. Yellow dung-flies swarm on the fresher deposits and fly up noisily when approached. The adults feed on other small flies, but their grubs feed on the dung itself. Beetles also play an important role in the removal and breakdown of animal dung and, by digging into cow-pats in various stages of decay, I found several different species. Two pairs of dor beetles were hard at work. These resemble the bloody-nosed beetle in shape and size, but they are much blacker and shinier and, in common with other dung beetles, they have broad, spiky front legs which they use for digging. They work in pairs, with the female digging a shaft up to two feet deep below the

bluebell

Some of the rich variety of flowers to be seen in the moist woodland close to Minterne Parva.

silverweed

herb robert

greater stitchwort

wood forget-me-not

cowslip

bloody nose beetle

MAY   The Cerne Valley, Dorset

cow-pat. The male digs in the dung itself and carries bundles down to the female. She then pushes it into chambers excavated on each side of the shaft and lays her eggs on it. The adult beetles fly strongly and often crash into cars at night.

The track leading down into Minterne Parva is bounded by well-grown hedges, in which I found dogwood, blackthorn, bramble, field maple, hazel and elder, in addition to the ubiquitous stinging nettle. Going by the now generally accepted theory that one shrub species signifies a century in the life of any thirty-yard stretch, these hedges are probably at least 400 years old. I noticed that they were alive with ichneumon flies searching for caterpillars in which to lay their eggs. Personally, I found not a single caterpillar, but the ichneumons have the advantage over us humans in that they hunt by scent. Having found a caterpillar, the female ich-neumon pierces it with her ovipositor and lays her eggs inside it. Her grubs feed inside the caterpillar, and by the time they are fully grown the caterpillar is nothing but a dead shell. The forage harvester had stopped work by the time I reached the meadow and several hares, easily seen now that the grass had been cut, were frolick-ing around it.

After turning right at the farm, the track runs between some fine old trees and drops into a moist, wooded area where a small stone bridge crosses a stream. The valley has cut right through the chalk here and is floored by the slightly older and very fertile Upper Greensand. Hart's tongue and polypody ferns grow on the bridge in company with herb robert. Mosses and liverworts abound on the wet ground, overhung by graceful sprays of pendulous sedge. Rhododendrons were coming into flower on the slightly higher ground when I was there, alongside a wonderful show of male ferns. Many of the latter are very old and the fresh green fronds were perched on tall pedestals formed by the old leaf bases.

The dried and empty 'shells' of the fungus BOVISTA NIGRESCENS *are common on the grassland. Related to the puffballs, the globular fruit bodies mature in autumn and then split open. They usually become detached from the soil and blow about in the wind, scattering spores as they go. The papery skins survive for many months and can be found at all times of the year.*

May is a great month for caterpillars, which have either hatched from their eggs or woken from their winter sleep. Careful examination of the vegetation will reveal large numbers, like these well-camouflaged caterpillars feeding on bush vetch.

I had fine views of Minterne House from the track as it passed through farm land just before turning down into the valley bottom and crossing another stream. A pair of pied wagtails were enjoying the feast of midges dancing over the water's edge here, and several goldfinches displayed their amazing agility as they clung to dandelion stems and tore out the developing seeds. Sturdy green and white spikes of the great horsetail sprouted from the soft ground. They looked more like miniature Christmas trees, with whorls of fine branches hugging the stems near the top, but the branches would soon elongate and give the plant a passing resemblance to a horse's tail. Beware of grasping these plants too strongly, for they are coated with silica crystals and can inflict painful cuts. They were once used for cleaning cooking pots and were known as scouring rushes, although they are more closely related to the ferns than to the true rushes.

germander speedwell

Bloody nose beetles abound in the herbage, feeding on various low-growing plants. When handled or otherwise alarmed, the beetle exudes a drop of blood from its mouth — hence its common name.

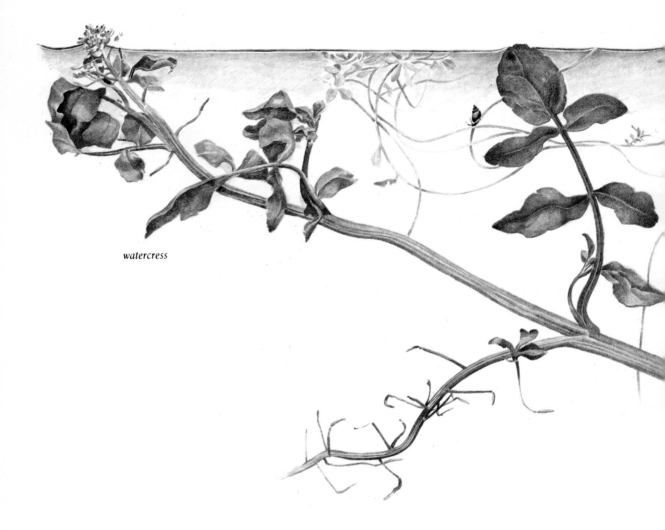

watercress

The clear stream babbling along by the road into Up Cerne is very alluring after a long walk, and even if you don't actually paddle it is well worth a stop to look at its teeming wildlife. Tufts of water moss spring from the gravelly bed, with scattered clumps of watercress growing in the muddier pockets near the edges, while the star-like leaves of water starwort form bright green patches at the surface. Freshwater shrimps scurry over the stream bed or swim on their sides as they dart from plant to plant. Numerous caddis fly larvae creep over the gravel and the vegetation, well protected in their cases of little stones or plant debris. Tiny hydra, like miniature sea anemones, cling to the water weeds, their dangling tentacles waiting to snare unwary water fleas and similar creatures. Close examination is necessary to see the fascinating hydra, and the best way to do this is to put a few pieces of water weed in some water in a jam jar or similar container — a polythene bag will do if you don't carry jam jars on your walks!

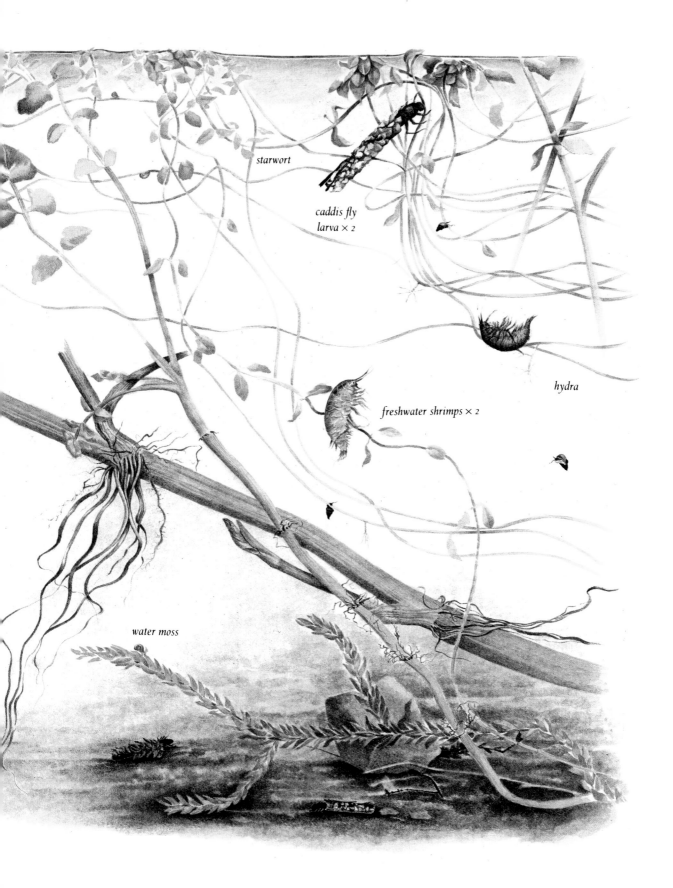

starwort

caddis fly
larva × 2

hydra

freshwater shrimps × 2

water moss

The Cerne Giant has watched over the valley and the
rolling hills to the west for some 1800 years. He is best
viewed in the afternoon from the A352, close to
its junction with the minor road leading into the village
(shown as 'Giant View' on map).

I turned left at the road, and after a short distance I turned right into an avenue of majestic limes. The leaves are a little past their best for eating at this time of year, but they still make an acceptable filling for a bread roll, especially if you have a little cream to put with them. Bearing left up the slope beyond the trees, I noticed two hares sunbathing in a small pit. I was able to get surprisingly close to them before they bounded away. Their long, black-tipped ears and black tails readily distinguished them from the rabbits I had seen on Giant Hill. Rabbits scuttle much closer to the ground, flashing a short white tail or 'scut' as they go.

Forking right soon after joining the bridleway at the top of Farm Hill, I was immediately aware of a change in the surroundings. There were no cattle here; and, although a few rabbits were still to be seen, the vegetation was quite different from that on Giant Hill. The grasses had grown tall and formed a sea of waving flower heads. Hairy oat and meadow oat were abundant, and here and there were bright yellowish-green patches of tor grass, an invasive and unpalatable species that frequently spreads over ungrazed chalk pasture. The fine-leaved fescues were still present, but less common and becoming crowded out by the more vigorous growth of the taller species. Soon these grasses themselves will be over-shadowed, for dense hawthorn scrub has already grown up and the lower slopes carry a dense thicket of ash and sycamore saplings.

The area is, of course, simply reverting to its natural state. Standing here and looking out at the softly rounded hills to the west, it is hard to believe that they were once clothed with forest. But there is no doubt about it: pollen grains preserved in peat and mud indicate that trees were the dominant plants all over the country until about 5000 years ago. Neolithic sites on the downs have yielded abundant charcoal derived from forest trees, and the same sites have produced shells of snails which today live only in the woodlands. The conversion of forests into grasslands was clearly the work of man and his animals. Timber was needed for building and for firewood, and woodland was also cleared to make way for sheep. Heavy grazing pressure kept the hillsides open for thousands of years, but now that grazing is much reduced the trees are beginning to come back.

A cleared area on the left of the path here supports dense patches of creeping thistle, and these plants in turn support vast numbers of white-lipped snails (*Cepaea hortensis*). I found many forms of this extremely variable snail: some with yellow shells and a few with pink shells, some with five brown bands, some with one brown band, and some with no bands at all. Thrushes and other birds always pick out the most obvious forms first, and so, as would be expected, the five-banded form was the most common in this rather scrubby habitat, where it has the best camouflage. Out on the open grassland the unbanded form is the most frequent, for its greenish-yellow colour blends well with the grasses. I examined a few of the snails on the ground below the thistles and soon found one with a brown woodlouse-like creature projecting from the shell. This was a young glow-worm enjoying a meal of meat and juices. It was nearly mature, and I can envisage the hillside gently glowing with greenish lights later in the year when the females turn on to attract their mates. The females are wingless and resemble the larvae, and it is difficult to believe that they are beetles, but the males are winged and more conventionally beetle-like.

Dropping down through the trees, I reached the road and found myself walking beside a crystal-clear stream. A few watercress plants grew in the shallow water, and figworts along the edges. Resisting the temptation to cool my feet in the bubbling water, I scooped a few handfuls of gravel from the bottom and put them into my empty sandwich box with some water and some water moss (*Fontinalis*) plucked from a submerged stone. As I watched, freshwater shrimps started to dart about, in company with mayfly and stonefly nymphs. Water snails, flatworms, and leeches were soon gliding around the sides of the box, and then the gravel itself seemed to move! I had actually scooped up a number of caddis larvae, which are well-known for their habit of building portable homes with pieces of gravel and other debris. I could see their heads and legs protruding from the fronts of the cases quite clearly. Each caddis larva builds its case to a specific design, and it is often possible to identify the species just by looking at its case.

Several adult caddis flies were resting on the low wall beside the stream, but my most exciting discovery concerned the mayflies. The nymphs of *Ephemera danica*, the largest British species, were fully grown and were emerging from the silt and swimming to the surface in some numbers. As soon as a nymph reached the surface, its skin split open and out came the adult, fully winged and able to fly away at once. The whole process was over in a second or so, but it was quite a spectacle, reminding me of rabbits emerging from a magician's hat. And the magic was not yet finished, for the mayflies were still not fully mature. The newly-emerged insects are dull and hairy – fishermen call them duns – and they still have one more skin-change. Some duns moult again within minutes of emergence, but *Ephemera* normally waits for a day or two. I was lucky enough to witness the final transformation of an insect clinging to a figwort leaf. A quick 'shiver' caused the skin to split along the back, and then the head, thorax, and legs were quickly withdrawn from this skin. Next it was the turn of the wings: slowly, but surely, the shiny wings of the true adult – the spinner – were dragged out of their hairy casings. The abdomen was withdrawn from the old skin at the same time and the insect took off for its short adult life, leaving a replica of itself in the form of the cast skin. No other group of insects undergoes such a moult after acquiring fully developed wings.

The lane winds its way back to Cerne Abbas by way of Upcerne, much of the journey being between fine hedgerows containing wild privet and gooseberry. Banks of germander speedwell seemed to reflect the blue sky. The Cerne Giant soon came into view, looking out over the Cerne Valley and wielding a club some 120 feet long. He is thought originally to have been associated with fertility rites – one look at his anatomy will explain why. His outline and features are formed by shallow trenches, about two feet wide, which are periodically cleaned – traditionally every seven years. Sheep graze the enclosure to keep the turf short.

I returned to my car by way of the stream, which has a much muddier bed here in Cerne Abbas. Water crowfoot is abundant, its hair-like leaves streaming out with the current and its attractive white flowers carpeting the slower-moving water near the banks. The cuckoo was still singing, but this time I spotted him – high in a dead elm and silhouetted sharply against the afternoon sky.

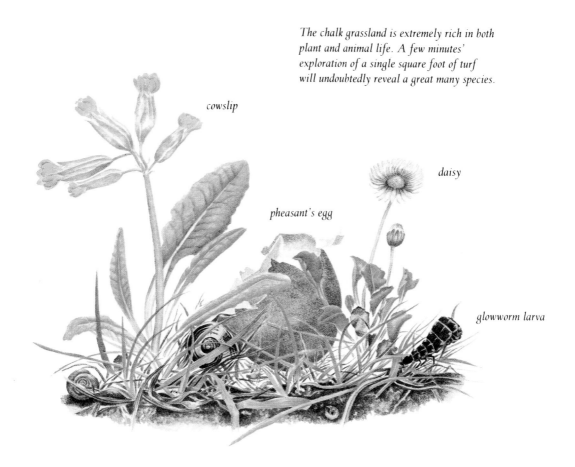

The chalk grassland is extremely rich in both plant and animal life. A few minutes' exploration of a single square foot of turf will undoubtedly reveal a great many species.

cowslip

daisy

pheasant's egg

glowworm larva

Summer
JUNE
Plockton and Loch Carron, Wester Ross

Scotland's north-west coast is a wild and beautiful region of rugged hills and extensive sea lochs. The lochs run essentially in an east-west direction, forming a much dissected coastline. They were gouged out of ancient rocks – actually some of the oldest in the world – by ice-age glaciers flowing down from the mountains. When the sea level rose after the ice age, as a result of the melting of enormous quantities of ice, the sea flooded the deeply-gouged valleys and formed the spectacular lochs that we see today. Steep hills rise straight up from the water in many places, and the alternation of hills and lochs all the way along the coast produces exciting panoramas combining land and sea.

Rainfall is high in this region – between fifty and eighty inches per year along most of the coast – but, under the influence of the North Atlantic Drift, the climate is relatively mild. Average temperatures are several degrees higher than those on the east coast, and in fact palm trees grow in some of the gardens. Much of the area is covered by blanket bog, which is an extensive layer of peat. Blanket bogs are characteristic of all high rainfall areas in Britain, especially in regions of acidic rocks. Relatively few plants can survive in these wet, acidic conditions, but the various kinds of bog mosses (*Sphagnum* species) positively revel in them. Dead plants decay very slowly in the waterlogged ground, and they gradually accumulate to form peat. Peat holds water like a sponge, and the mosses continue to grow on its surface, slowly increasing the depth of the blanket. In some places it is over five metres deep. Several sedges also contribute to the peat formation. Blanket bogs are rather infertile habitats because most of the nutrient minerals are locked up in the undecayed peat, but heathers flourish in such conditions and most parts of the region are dominated by heather moors. The climate is also ideal for tree growth, and where the bogs have been drained and fertilized there are some extensive coniferous plantations. Red squirrels, pine martens, and wild cats live in these forests.

The walk described here is based on the secluded village of Plockton, nestling on the northern edge of Lochalsh and looking out over the mouth of Loch Carron. It is said to be one of the most photographed villages in Scotland. Protected on the north and west by a rugged promontory known as the 'plock', it has a fine natural harbour

58

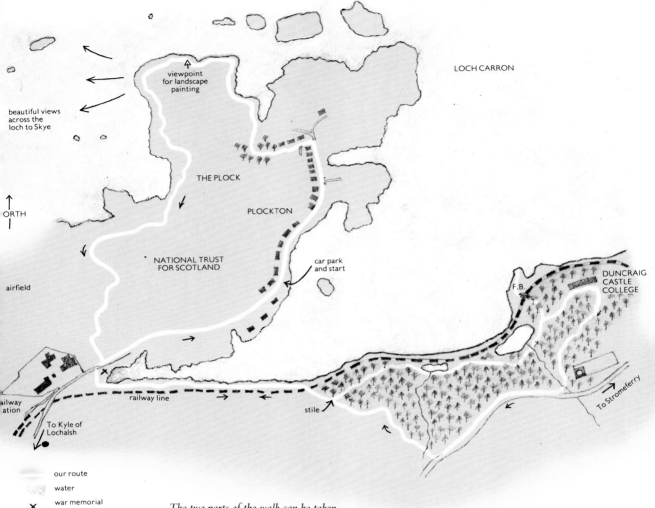

LOCH CARRON

viewpoint
for landscape
painting

beautiful views
across the
loch to Skye

THE PLOCK

PLOCKTON

ORTH

NATIONAL TRUST
FOR SCOTLAND

car park
and start

airfield

DUNCRAIG
CASTLE
COLLEGE

F.B.

To Stromeferry

railway
ation

railway line

stile

To Kyle of
Lochalsh

⎓⎓⎓ our route

water

× war memorial

F.B. footbridge

The two parts of the walk can be taken together or separately. There is no set length to the first part, which takes in the coastal moorland, but it is a minimum of $3\frac{1}{4}$ miles. The second part is about 3 miles long. The going is tough for much of the walk, with very irregular terrain. Waterproof footwear is recommended for the first part of the walk at least, and waterproof clothing is useful for the second part if rain has fallen recently.

Refreshments can be obtained in Plockton.

Cars can be parked either in the sea-front car park (Map Ref: NG 803333) or, for the second part of the walk, near the station.

You can begin the walk at almost any time of day, for it is light until after 11 pm up here in June, but it is best to avoid the moorland part in the evening. This is when the midges are at their most troublesome.

Overleaf: Sunset over the Applecross Peninsula and the mouth of Loch Carron, seen from the northern tip of the plock. Rugged and almost treeless, the Applecross Peninsula, two miles across the water from Plockton, has some truly spectacular scenery which can now be appreciated to the full from a new road winding through the hills to a height of over 2000 feet.

and some superb views across the water to the surrounding hills. It was once a crofting community, with the houses grouped on the plock, but when Sir Hugh Innes bought the village in 1801 he cleared the plock and built the present village down on the shore. Plockton has changed hands several times since then and was once a flourishing fishing port, but it is now just a quiet summer resort.

The walk is in two distinct parts and, as well as providing splendid views of the scenery, it allows the walker to explore the moorland of the plock and the lush greenery of the planted woodlands to the south. The long hours of daylight in this region in the summer are an added bonus for walker and naturalist alike.

I began my walk at Plockton's tiny sea-front car park and, accompanied by the tinkling of the rigging on boats moored in the bay, made my way along the main street, admiring the neat houses and the palm trees in their sea-front gardens on the opposite side of the road. Beyond the islets strewn over the bay rose the rugged, tree-clad tongue of land separating Loch Carron from Loch Kishorn, while Duncraig Castle stood high above the southern shoreline, surrounded by majestic pines and the green and mauve of a rhododendron forest. Castle Crags towered up behind the castle to form an imposing barrier.

Turning left at the end of the road, I passed the camp site and walked between colourful banks of wild roses as I made for the rocky headlands of the plock that rises up on the north and west of the village. Most of this area is owned by the National Trust for Scotland and is now delightfully wild. The greater part of it is clothed with blanket bog and supports moorland vegetation, although there are some bare rocks and a few clumps of small trees. The rocks are Torridonian Sandstones, laid down well over 600 million years ago. There are no proper footpaths over the plock, but there are plenty of well-trodden tracks, and several prominent landmarks ensure that one cannot get lost – as long as the mist keeps away! The sun was shining as I reached the slopes, and warm enough for several bikini-clad girls to brighten up the grey rocks, but cloud is rarely far away in the Highlands and I was aware of a thick mist already descending on the mountains of the Applecross Peninsula just over the water.

On reaching the first rocky slopes, I was faced with the choice of going down to the shore or climbing to the top. A narrow path rising through rocks on my right looked inviting, and so I chose the higher route. Scrubby birches and rowans brushed against me as I climbed the rough path, and there were also a few small oaks – very near their northern limit here at Plockton. Bilberry and common cow-wheat sprouted from the rock crevices, while the hollows were filled with squelchy bog mosses. The peaty soil was very apparent as I reached the top and emerged on to the

The rugged cliffs of the plock, brightly decorated with thrift and other flowers in June, afford fine views across the mouth of Loch Carron. Seals often bask on the off-shore rocks and islands at low tide, and the cliffs are also good spots for bird watchers. In the distance are the hills of the Applecross Peninsula.

thrift or sea pink

meadow pipit

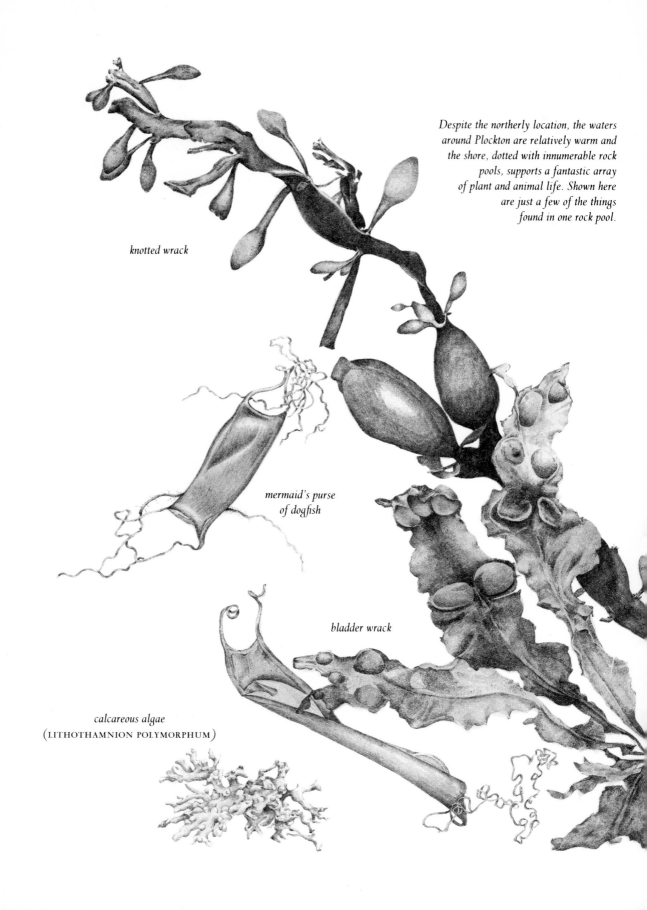

knotted wrack

Despite the northerly location, the waters around Plockton are relatively warm and the shore, dotted with innumerable rock pools, supports a fantastic array of plant and animal life. Shown here are just a few of the things found in one rock pool.

mermaid's purse of dogfish

bladder wrack

calcareous algae
(LITHOTHAMNION POLYMORPHUM)

north-facing slope. Heather and crowberry grow here in abundance, and tormentil flowers peeped out from the rough turf like hundreds of little yellow eyes. The fluffy white fruiting heads of cotton grass swayed gently in the breeze, in contrast to the stiff and elegant spikes of the heath spotted orchids. And all around was the aromatic scent of the bog myrtle, whose greyish-leaved bushes are dotted right across this moorland habitat.

The rocky promontory provides superb views of the many off-shore islets, and away to the west I could just make out the dim shapes of the mountains of Skye. Nearer at hand, assorted gulls filled the air with noisy calls as they displayed their astonishing aeronautic abilities along the edge of the cliff. Meadow pipits and the somewhat larger and greyer rock pipits bounced and tumbled over the rocks and vegetation as they gathered up the midges.

The uneven terrain, with several sharp drops, makes it difficult to walk far on this northernmost part of the plock, and I retraced my steps through the birches and rowans to head westwards down a grassy slope towards the sea. The creamy white spikes of several lesser butterfly orchids poked up through the grass, and dense clumps of yellow irises revelled in the damp conditions closer to the shore.

The tide was well out and I was able to explore the rocks, although a thick carpet of bladder wrack and other brown seaweeds made walking somewhat perilous. Mussels, barnacles and massive limpets clung to the rocks above the level of the seaweeds, and scattered all over the bay were the beautiful pink shells, or tests, of the edible sea urchin.

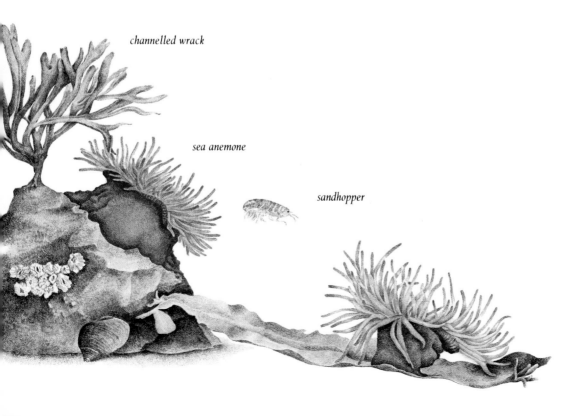

channelled wrack

sea anemone

sandhopper

Utterly fascinating were the numerous rock pools, which can be found all around
the northern and western shores of the plock at low tide. They were full of colourful
sea anemones and delicate red seaweeds, among which I found a variety of molluscs
and small crustaceans. The uppermost rocks of the shore and the surrounding
cliffs were painted pink in many places by the carpets of thrift, or sea pink, which was
in full flower. Elsewhere, they carried extensive patches of bright orange lichens
and the pale, star-like flowers of the English stonecrop.

My binoculars revealed several groups of common seals basking on the exposed
rocks fringing the off-shore islets. They would probably remain there until the tide
floated them off again, for seals are not the most athletic of beasts on land, and where
they have to haul out on to rocks they often take up position before the tide recedes
and simply wait there until it returns. Grey seals, recognized by their more pointed
muzzles, also visit these shores, but I did not see any myself. A red-throated diver
swam quietly along with just its head and neck showing – rather like a submarine's
periscope – and then disappeared completely on an underwater fishing trip.

It is possible to walk right round the plock on the shore at low tide, but the rocky
terrain and seaweeds make it hard going. There is also a risk of being cut off by the
returning tide, for there are few points at which one can scale the cliffs. I preferred to
do my walking on the plateau and, after exploring just one bay, I climbed up through
the bracken and the rowans and birches which here come right down to the shore.

The plateau is very wet in places, especially in the central hollow, from which peat
has clearly been dug at various times. Several smooth newts, which had presumably
been breeding in the scattered pools, dragged themselves over the sodden bog
mosses. The hollow supports a colony of cotton grass so dense that the fluffy heads
resembled a small snow field. Other plants on the wetter part of the plateau include
bog asphodel and cross-leaved heath – a pale-flowered relative of the bell heather
which gets its name because its tiny leaves occur in fours and spread out rather like
the arms of a cross. The most fascinating of the bog plants, however, are the insect-
eating sundews, which trap small insects to augment the meagre mineral supplies
they obtain from the peat. The sundew's leaves are clothed with modified hairs, each
of which bears a blob of sticky fluid. The latter sparkles in the sunshine and attracts
flies and other insects, which become hopelessly entangled. Stimulated by the
struggles of a trapped insect, and also by its 'taste', the sundew leaf gradually curls up
and enfolds the victim. Digestive juices pour out from the leaf surface and the insect
is slowly dissolved. The resulting fluids are absorbed by the leaf, which later uncurls
to reveal just a few pieces of the insect's horny skeleton. The hairs, or tentacles, are
re-charged with sticky fluid and the leaf is then open for business again. I found two
species of sundew at Plockton – the round-leaved sundew, whose leaves resemble
tiny salt spoons, and the great sundew, with elongated leaves looking more like

Herons patrol the shallows all round the plock, while oystercatchers (below) are conspicuous on the shore at low tide.

spoon handles. Both species were in flower in June, but their flowers are small and white and far less conspicuous than the glistening reddish leaves.

The drier parts of the plateau carry various grasses and clumps of heather and bell heather, with the delicate pink spikes of heath spotted orchids and lousewort poking up here and there among them. The lousewort is a semi-parasitic species which attaches itself to the roots of grasses and withdraws water and minerals from them. On the west side of the plateau, close to the road and the airstrip, there is a dense forest of gorse bushes. The airstrip was constructed in 1966 and enables the region to be served by an air ambulance, although most of the planes using it today are private ones belonging to holiday-makers. The strip's wind-sock is visible from most parts of the plock and is a useful landmark. By heading for it, you can easily pick up the road which leads back to the village. But I preferred a shorter route and, with my back to the wind-sock and the white school buildings away to my right, I aimed for the highest point on the plock. A seat has been provided here for those who wish to rest their legs or simply to admire the splendid views. From the seat I followed the well-worn trail that runs in a southerly direction to meet the road by the war memorial.

I decided to break my walk here and return to the village for a musical interlude, for I had heard that the Scottish Chamber Orchestra was giving an open-air concert that afternoon. The setting was delightful, on a small island easily reached on foot at low tide, and the music was enjoyed by a remarkably large audience for such a small and remote place. It's not every concert that ends with the words: 'This must be our last number because the tide is coming in.'

Some of the colourful plants and animals found
on the rocks and heathland of the plock. The
harestail cotton grass is one of two similar
species growing there. Each stalk has one flower
cluster, which becomes white and fluffy in fruit.
The common cotton grass usually has three or
more clusters on each stem.

damsel fly

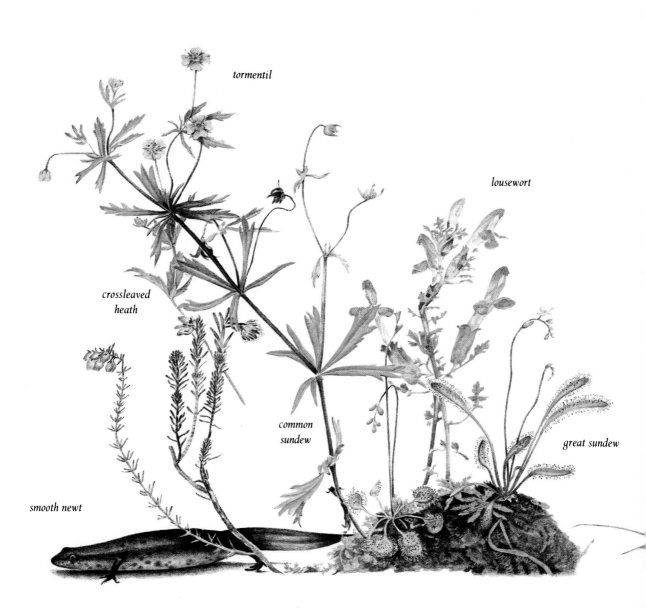

tormentil

lousewort

crossleaved
heath

common
sundew

great sundew

smooth newt

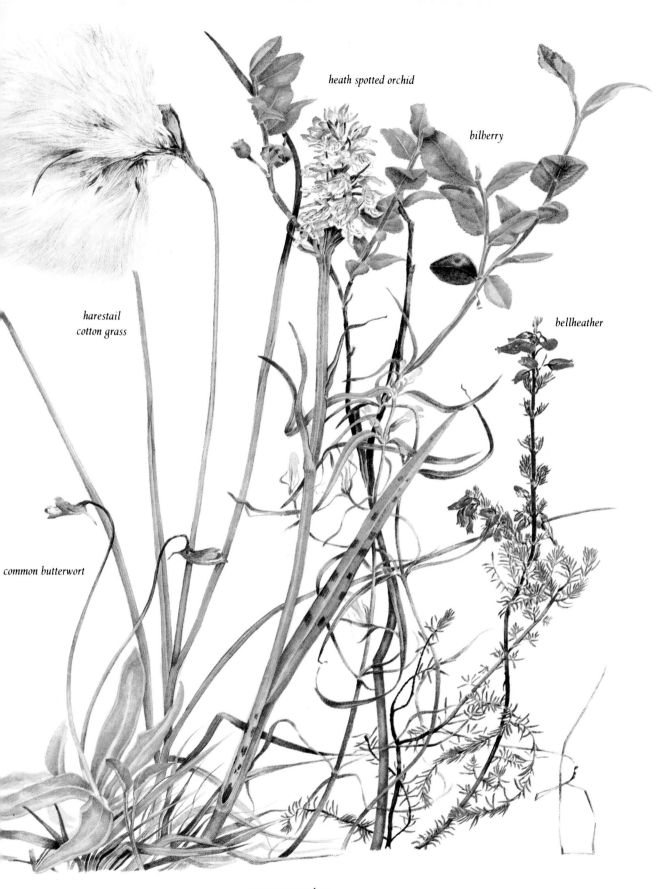

heath spotted orchid

bilberry

harestail
cotton grass

bellheather

common butterwort

common cow wheat

I did not actually re-start my walk until the middle of the following day, after some very heavy rain. I returned to the war memorial and, just beyond it, took the footpath leading down to the head of the narrow inlet. More clumps of yellow irises grow here where fresh water seeps down the slopes, and the flowers were alive with long-snouted hover-flies (*Rhingia campestris*). The insects paid no attention to me, although I was only inches from them, and were literally queueing up to crawl into the nectar-filled tubes formed by the outer petals and the strange, petal-like stigmas.

I followed the path along the south of the inlet. It was low tide again and the gulls were busy scavenging in the dense beds of bladder wrack and channelled wrack. Winkles were abundant among these seaweeds. What looks like a coat of tar or black paint on the rocks close to high tide level is in fact the very common coastal lichen called *Verrucaria maura*. Large patches of crusty white lichens grow on the rocks fringing the seaward side of the path, together with prominent tufts of *Ramalina siliquosa*, a greyish-green lichen often known as sea ivory. Pink cushions of thrift also decorate the edges of the path in summer, while carpets of scurvy-grass – a white-flowered crucifer – cover the shingle.

On the landward side of the path the rocky banks support heather and bilberry and numerous ferns, studded with the flowers of tormentil and overhung by birches and rhododendrons. But to my mind the most fascinating plants here are the map lichens (*Rhizocarpon* species), which completely cover the exposed rocks with patterns of greys, greens and browns. Each colony has a thin black border, and where neighbouring colonies meet their borders look just like boundaries drawn on a map.

Plockton's houses gradually came into view as I walked along the inlet, and I could see why it is so often photographed. Even with the tide out and large stretches of muddy and stony shore exposed, it remains bright and clean, and with the hills rising protectively behind the houses it radiates peace and tranquility. When the tide is in and the houses are reflected in the water it makes a fairy-tale scene. I continued along the progressively more rugged path and, after passing under the railway line, found myself in a small canyon. Maidenhair spleenwort and polypody ferns peered out from the rock crevices, while dense clumps of male fern and great woodrush clothed the ground. Hard fern was also noticeable, its slender fertile fronds standing stiffly to attention above the more or less prostrate sterile fronds. This bright green species is sometimes known as the fishbone fern or the ladder fern because of the regular and often rung-like branching of its fertile fronds. A cotoneaster, more commonly seen fanning out over cottage walls and fences, sprawled over a rock, owing its life in the wild to some unknown bird who dropped a seed from the overhead wires.

Oaks and pines stood over me as I climbed the path above the railway line, and all the time the views of Plockton were getting more spectacular as the waterfront panorama unfolded. And then I crossed a ladder-like stile on the left and plunged

A branch of western hemlock, a North American tree which is now widely planted in Britain. It grows especially in the mild, damp climate along the west coast of Scotland and there are several magnificent specimens around Duncraig Castle.

into a rhododendron thicket. The leaves and branches were still dripping with water after the rain and I was soon decidedly damp, but the flowers were magnificent. The bumble bees thought so, too, and there was a constant hum in the air as they flew from flower to flower in search of nectar. Steam rose from the thicket as the sun evaporated the water, and the atmosphere was like that of a tropical forest.

The path drops down through the rhododendrons and I suddenly found myself staring at a large patch of seaweed. The railway embankment runs right along the waterfront here and a small arch designed to allow a stream to reach the sea also allows the high tide to sweep over this low-lying area behind the embankment. Thrift flowers formed a pink border to this marine enclave, and I found several sea urchin tests among the rocks and seaweeds. There were also some sea anemones clinging to the rocks close to the arch in the embankment. Beyond this enclave, the massive fireplace of a ruined house conjured up visions of an enormous log fire at Christmas, and then came a much more sinister-looking chimney rising up from some kind of oven! I discovered later that it is an old incinerator dating from the castle's wartime role as a hospital.

I turned left just after these ruins and headed back towards the railway. Turning right when I reached it, I then skirted another marine enclave and emerged from the woodland on to a tarmac road. I turned left here and, crossing a little bridge, looked down on a tiny railway station, Duncraig Halt. It is on the Highland Line, joining Kyle of Lochalsh and Inverness, the most northerly railway on the west coast. The western half of this line, through Glen Carron and all the way along the bank of Loch Carron, is one of the most beautiful rail routes in Britain.

Beyond the station bridge, the path continues to a little jetty on the shore. This is well worth a visit for the marvellous views across the mouth of Loch Carron to the Applecross Mountains behind. Stark pines grow on several of the islets in the loch, and a number of herons were flapping around them as I looked out over the shining waters. Some eider ducks drifted casually past the nearest islet, and in the distance I could see more seals basking on the rocks.

I retraced my steps to the bridge and followed the road past the elegant Duncraig Castle. Built by Sir Alexander Matheson late in the nineteenth century, the castle stands on a bluff overlooking the mouth of Loch Carron. It became a school in the 1930s and was used as a hospital during the war. It is now a catering college. Many fine exotic trees grow in the grounds, together with some equally majestic Scots pines. The surrounding woodlands are said to have been planted at one time with at least one specimen of every tree known to be able to grow in this Scottish climate. A little further along the road, just past The Square, stands a tall wellingtonia, recognizable by its soft red bark which can be punched with impunity.

Turning right on to the Plockton-Stromeferry road, I admired the giant Sitka spruces on the right and the western hemlocks on the left. Beyond these imported giants there is an attractive avenue of oaks and beeches, whose trunks are clothed with the beautiful green lungwort lichen (*Lobaria pulmonaria*). This species is very susceptible to atmospheric pollution and has disappeared from many parts of Britain, but it is still quite common in western areas. Many small animals were roaming the damp lichen in search of food after the rain. A quick count over about a hundred square centimetres revealed two slugs, two small worms, a crane-fly, a woodlouse and a snipe-fly. The latter, a handsome yellow and brown insect, sat in its characteristic head-down attitude, which has given it the name of 'down-looker-fly'.

A little further up the road I crossed a stile on the right. The sun shone brightly on the birch-dotted field beside the path and several pearl-bordered fritillary butterflies were enjoying its warmth. I then entered a wooded area with deep carpets of hair moss under the oaks. A miniature forest of spore capsules sprang from the carpet and most of the capsules were about to shed their pointed pixie hoods in readiness to scatter their spores. The delicate feather moss (*Thuidium tamariscinum*) covered the bases of many trees, while the pale green rosettes of butterwort were prominent on the damper parts of the path as it dropped down towards the coast. Some of the rosettes were crowned by their solitary purple flowers, which resemble violets at first sight. The butterwort is another insectivorous plant, although less spectacular than the sundew. It is found in all kinds of wet places, but is especially common around wet rocks. Its leaves are coated with sticky fluid which traps small insects, and a successful leaf gradually digests its victim.

The path led me back to the stile by the rhododendrons, and from there I had to retrace my steps to Plockton. But I did not tire of the splendid scenery, and spotted several plants and insects that I had missed on the way out. And there was still one surprise in store: as I neared the railway bridge a roebuck leapt across the path just in front of me. I don't know who got the greater fright.

Summer
JULY
Lathkill Dale, Derbyshire

Derbyshire's Peak District is an outstandingly beautiful upland region at the southern end of the Pennines. It contains some of England's finest scenery, and most of it is included in the Peak National Park – the first national park to be designated in Britain, in 1950. There are two markedly contrasting areas here, generally known as the White Peak and the Dark Peak. The White Peak, occupying the central part of the District, is formed by the pale grey Carboniferous Limestone. It is essentially a plateau landscape of green fields and pale stone walls, dissected by numerous steep-sided valleys, or dales. The Dark Peak surrounds the White Peak like a horse-shoe on the north, east, and west. It is formed by the Millstone Grit – much harder and slightly younger than the Carboniferous Limestone – and it is essentially a moorland landscape. Its inner boundaries are marked in many places by precipitous cliffs known locally as edges. There is a reminder of the importance of the Millstone Grit at every entrance to the park on a major road, for the boundaries are marked with millstones. Although no longer used for millstones, the grit is still worked for building stone.

The Peak National Park is well supplied with car parks, from which you can embark on some superb country walks. The route described here is entirely within the White Peak area, although you get a glimpse of the Dark Peak at one point and can compare the two landscapes. The White Peak plateau has been farmed for many centuries and is now a very artificial habitat with relatively few plant species, but the steep-sided dales have been little affected by agriculture and support some extremely rich woodland and grassland habitats. The walk enables you to see both wild and farmed areas, beginning with the beauty of Lathkill Dale.

Cut deeply into the limestone, the dale was once a busy lead-mining centre, but the mining had only a limited effect on the natural community and the area is now a National Nature Reserve. A public footpath runs through the reserve, enabling visitors to enjoy the abundant wildlife in this amazingly quiet and peaceful wooded valley.

74

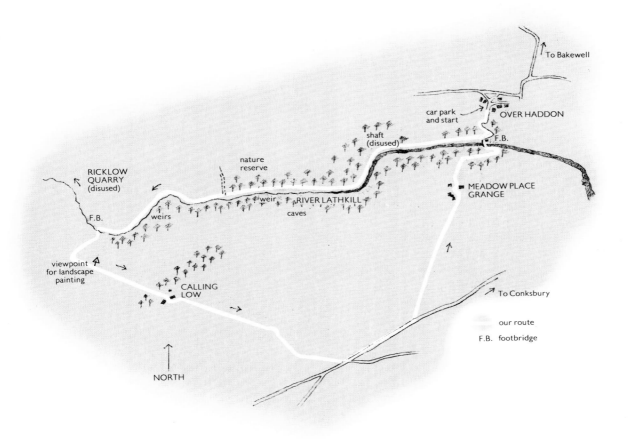

The walk is about 5 miles long and, apart from the haul out of Cales Dale, is quite easy going. Normal walking shoes should be adequate except after prolonged rain, when the dale can be very muddy. The walk can be started in the morning or the afternoon.

Refreshments are not available on the route of the walk, but drinks can sometimes be obtained at Calling Low Farm.

There is a large car park in Over Haddon (Map Ref: SK 203665) and there is also room for a few cars by the side of the road just above Lathkill Lodge.

Overleaf: The view north from just below Calling Low Farm. The extensive pastures and meadows of the White Peak plateau are clearly seen, together with many miles of the dry-stone walls that enclose them. Equally prominent are the massive limestone shelves forming the northern wall of Lathkill Dale, which stretches away to the right in the middle distance.

JULY *Lathkill Dale, Derbyshire*

A bright yellow roof greeted me as I walked down through the trees to meet the
river at Lathkill Lodge. It was not a new kind of tiling, but the roof of an old mill
covered with biting stonecrop in full flower. Patches of herb robert among the
stonecrop contributed to a most attractive 'thatch' and gave a foretaste of what was
to be a very colourful walk. Entering the Lathkill Dale Reserve, I was immediately
treated to drifts of the beautiful violet-blue flowers of the meadow cranesbill. This
striking plant grows in a variety of grassy places, but is usually confined to limestone
and it is at its best on the Pennines of Derbyshire and Yorkshire. Here in Lathkill Dale
it forms great clumps along the river bank. Other flowering plants enjoying the
moist, rich soil of the valley floor include hemp agrimony, meadowsweet, great
willowherb and hogweed. The flowers of the hogweed expose their nectar freely on
the surface and attract huge numbers of flies and other insects. Many a drama has
been enacted on the broad stage of a hogweed flower-head, for not all the insect
visitors are peaceful nectar-sippers: several of the flies are highwaymen, lurking there
only to grab smaller species and to rob them of their life-blood. I witnessed several
such performances during my walk.

False oat grass is common on both sides of the path and I watched the purple
anthers scattering clouds of pollen as they swung freely in the breeze. The most
abundant plant on the river bank, however, is reed canary-grass, whose pale green
leaves and flower spikes seem to be constantly whispering as the breeze brushes over
them. The plant grows right by the water's edge, forming dense stands up to four
feet high, and actually covers a large part of the river bed. The river itself was almost
non-existent, the only water I could see being a few shrinking pools dotted over its
stony bed. But this is quite normal during the summer, when most of the water
sinks into the limestone and continues its journey through old mine workings and
other subterranean channels before re-surfacing below Lathkill Lodge. The rocks and
boulders exposed on the river bed were thickly clothed with various mosses, and
springing up between them were dense beds of fool's watercress. The leaves of this
plant are very similar to those of the true watercress, which grows with it here in
Lathkill Dale, but the two plants are unrelated. Fool's watercress is an umbellifer and
can easily be recognized when in flower by its umbrella-shaped flower-heads. It is
often picked and eaten, apparently without ill-effect, in mistake for the true
watercress.

Alders and willows are scattered here and there along the valley floor, but the
main trees of Lathkill Dale are the ash and the wych elm. These two species clothe
the steep southern side of the dale. The northern side, stretching up on my right as I
walked, is less steep and carries scrub-invaded grassland. Hawthorn is the main
shrub, but much more eye-catching are the abundant wild roses, which were in full
flower at the time of my visit. Cascades of pale pink flowers tumbled over the other
vegetation, and countless fallen petals mingled with those of the meadow cranesbill

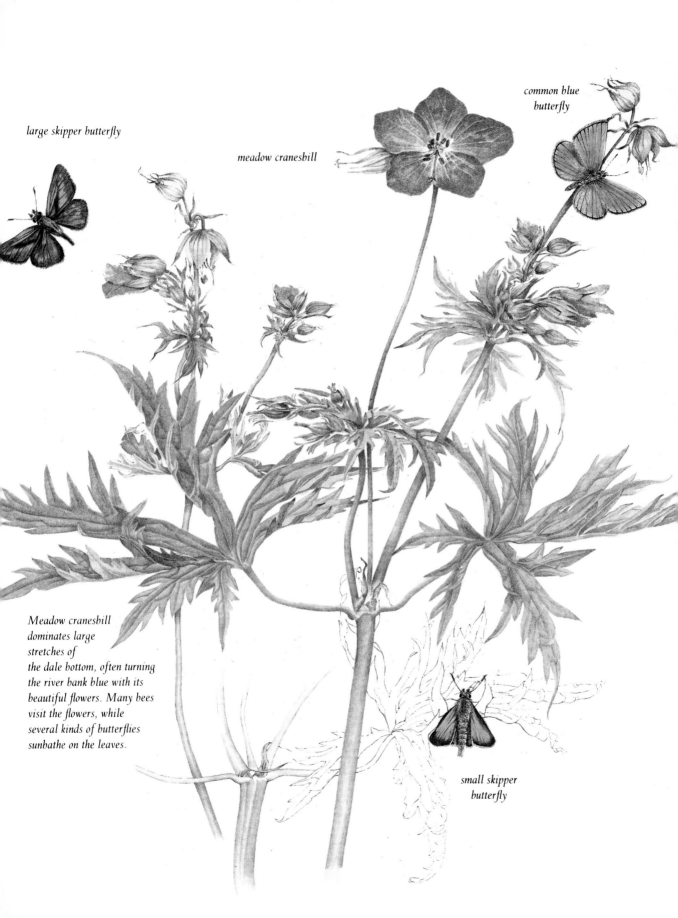

large skipper butterfly

meadow cranesbill

common blue butterfly

Meadow cranesbill
dominates large
stretches of
the dale bottom, often turning
the river bank blue with its
beautiful flowers. Many bees
visit the flowers, while
several kinds of butterflies
sunbathe on the leaves.

small skipper
butterfly

along the edges of the path. The south-facing (northern) side of the dale also carries
many natural rock gardens, created wherever the hard grey limestone breaks
through the turf. Among the many fascinating plants which I found growing in the
fissures and on the ledges were biting stonecrop, crosswort, shining cranesbill,
dovesfoot cranesbill, wild thyme, marjoram, rockrose and mouse-ear hawkweed – all
with yellow or pinkish flowers and forming beautiful patterns on the grey limestone.
Wall rue and maidenhair spleenwort ferns were also common, and nearly every
crevice sheltered a long-legged harvestman.

   Rabbits are abundant in the dale and, free from persecution, they are relatively

The dale has a large rabbit population and the animals can be seen casually grazing by the path at all times of day and night. They are not shy and are quite happy to be photographed at close range.

bold. Several of them sat calmly drinking from the puddles and munching the lush vegetation at the side of the path, and did not move until I was within a few yards. Even then, they did not move far – just a short way up the bank towards their burrows. Birds were noticeably busy all along the dale as parents strove to collect enough food for their broods, many of which were about to leave their nests and were demanding ever-increasing supplies of nourishment. One large willow overhanging the river seemed to be a particularly good source of food: a pair of nuthatches were exploring every crevice for insects and other small creatures, and I watched their comings and goings for a full ten minutes, during which time they made at least three trips back to the nest with beaks overflowing with tasty morsels. They were joined by a tree-creeper as I watched and he (or she) also had no difficulty in digging plenty of food from the trunk.

Between the path and the river there is a narrow stone-lined channel – the 'tail' of the Mandale Mine Sough, which carried away the water that was pumped out of the mine. It joins the river about 250 yards west of the gateway by Lathkill Lodge. Water still flows along this channel in winter. The tail disappears into a tunnel – the sough – close to where the path enters the woods, and the remains of the Mandale Mine Engine House can be seen on the right.

The Mandale Mine is mentioned as a source of lead in a document dated 1288 AD, and it was probably in production long before that – possibly as early as Roman times. But mechanization did not come until 1840, when a waterwheel, about thirty-five feet in diameter, was installed to drive the pumps needed to keep the mine free from water. The water needed to drive the wheel was brought from higher up the dale by means of a narrow canal, or leat. The engine house was built in 1847, and the waterwheel was replaced by a steam engine in 1848. Lead production soared with

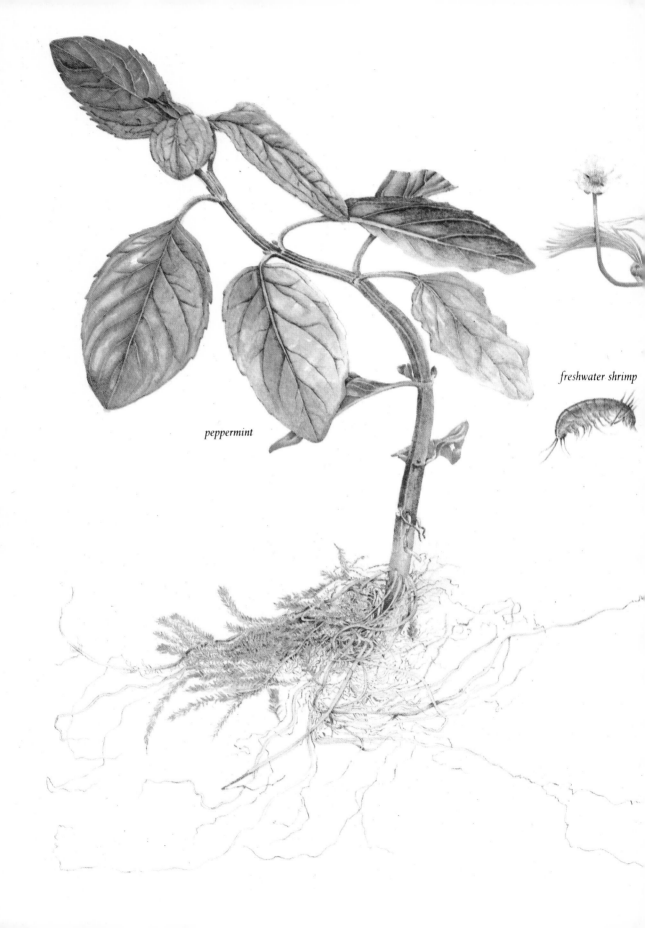

peppermint

freshwater shrimp

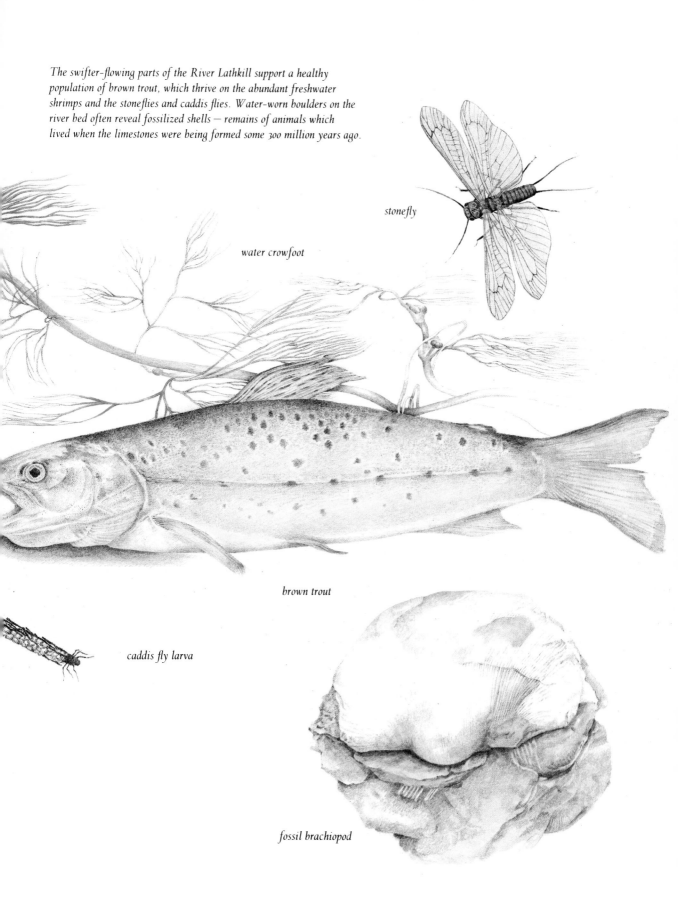

The swifter-flowing parts of the River Lathkill support a healthy population of brown trout, which thrive on the abundant freshwater shrimps and the stoneflies and caddis flies. Water-worn boulders on the river bed often reveal fossilized shells — remains of animals which lived when the limestones were being formed some 300 million years ago.

stonefly

water crowfoot

brown trout

caddis fly larva

fossil brachiopod

these innovations, but it lasted only a few years and work ceased in Mandale Mine in 1852. The engine house is now in ruins, but you can clearly see the large pit by the side of it which was the site of the waterwheel. Many of the mine workings are now in a dangerous state and, although the various openings may look tempting, on no account should you try to explore them.

The immediate surroundings of the mine have obviously been greatly disturbed over the years and sycamore has now become established in place of the native ash and elm. This invasive species, probably introduced from southern Europe by the Romans, occurs in several other parts of the woodland and a good deal of effort is being expended by the Nature Conservancy Council to reduce its numbers and encourage the regeneration of ash and elm. By leafing early and casting a dense shade, the sycamore reduces the variety of the ground flora, and it is also avoided by most of our birds and other animals. It was noticeable that the ground cover increased as I passed from the sycamores to the more natural woodland of the dale. Dog's mercury dominates the ground in most areas and I found that it sheltered an

immense population of the harvestman *Phalangium opilio.* They were resting on the leaves and not easy to spot from a distance, but they must have formed a formidable horde as they went hunting for other small animals by night. Many would undoubtedly succumb to their stronger brethren, for the harvestmen are not averse to cannibalism.

A short way beyond the mine I passed the remains of the aqueduct that once carried the water for the waterwheel across the river. The wooden troughs that held the water have long since disappeared, but the remains of several stone pillars have been preserved by the Peak District Mines Historical Society. Walking by the water, I could see the river's huge brown trout population becoming more and more agitated as the pools shrank. The fishes darted this way and that in futile attempts to escape, but a rescue mission had already been mounted and the fishes were being carefully netted and taken to safer waters further down the dale. Several grey wagtails took advantage of the commotion to capture the numerous midges and other insects that were being disturbed. Bird activity continued unabated amongst the trees as well. A

A stoat emerged from the dense grass on the river bank, observed us suspiciously, and then disappeared without a sound.

young robin ticked noisily when I dared to approach his low perch, while chaffinches and greenfinches scoured the woodland floor for seeds and insects. A family of great tits were also busily searching the ground and the undergrowth for food, and making a great deal of noise about it. Their shrill and rapidly-repeated calls of *tsee-tsee-tsee-tsee*, which are primarily contact calls designed to keep the party together, carried far through the woodland.

I continued along the path, past dense patches of the elegant wood melick grass. Pink mounds of herb robert and shining cranesbill covered the numerous spoil heaps which, together with some large hollows, mark the site of the Lathkill Dale Mine. Colourful spikes of lords-and-ladies berries poked up amongst the dog's mercury and other herbage, while grey squirrels scampered up and down the tree trunks. I emerged from the woodland close to a small dam, which was originally constructed to provide the head of water necessary to feed the leat running to the Mandale Mine waterwheel. It also provided water for a wheel at the Lathkill Dale Mine. The dam was in the sunlight and it was an ideal spot to rest and view the superb scenery. The steep southern side of the dale is densely wooded beyond the dam, although I could just see the grassy plateau right at the top, but the northern side carries lightly grazed grassland punctuated

dabchick and young

by stone walls and occasional limestone scars and patches of scree. Among the many flowering plants on these grassy slopes are rockrose, salad burnet, marjoram, wild thyme and the tiny fairy flax. Quaking grass, or totters, is also quite common, but on the steeper slopes, where grazing pressure is slight, false oat grass is the dominant plant. This tall and rather elegant grass, recognized by its shiny flower-heads, is one of the first plants to colonize patches of scree – along with the ubiquitous herb robert.

Above the dam, the river is wide and, with little flow, it virtually becomes a lake. Drifts of water crowfoot flowers painted the lake white around the edges, while much of the deeper water was carpeted with the floating leaves of the broad-leaved pondweed. A little grebe, or dabchick, had to work hard to feed three hungry youngsters and she spent more time below the surface than on top of it. I could never predict where she was going to surface, but her offspring were never far away when she surfaced with a beakful of small animals for them to eat. A mallard duck had an easier time, for her brood of ducklings could feed themselves. Several moorhens also swam jerkily over the water, occasionally disturbing the peace with a harsh *kurruck*. Closer at hand, as I perched on the wall of the dam, I watched the emergence of some large stoneflies. Fat nymphs struggled out of the water and crawled up the stones, where, after a short rest, the skins split open and out crawled the winged adults. They needed to harden their wings before they could fly away.

Numerous grasshoppers struggled from their nymphal skins on the surrounding grassland, clinging tightly to the grasses while their new skins and wings hardened. Common blue and large skipper butterflies were also emerging from their pupae in large numbers and sitting in the sun with their wings wide open, decorating the grass like colourful jewels.

It was with some reluctance that I dragged myself away from this delightful spot and continued along the waterside path. The grasshoppers on the sun-drenched slope were already well dried and the males were chirping away like clocks ticking at vastly increased speeds. The 'song', which is designed to attract the female, is produced by rubbing the back legs against the wings, and it is easy to see the male in action by homing in on the sound. Ravenous hordes of small tortoiseshell butterfly caterpillars were stripping the leaves from the stinging nettles at the side of the path.

Massive grey limestones tower up like terraces on the right. I watched jackdaws disporting themselves on up-currents around the face of the cliff, while several redstarts darted to and fro over the lower scree slopes and snapped up flies and other insects in mid-air. This handsome summer visitor often nests in old stone walls and rock crevices and the Dales are very much to its liking.

The valley closes in again beyond the cliffs, although the southern slope becomes less steep, and the path becomes rougher as it climbs steadily westwards through fast-developing ash scrub. I was struck by the intense green of this narrow part of the dale, with the river now just a trickle running between the moss-covered boulders and the watercress – a truly idyllic spot. I crossed the little footbridge and picked my way along the rough path that winds through tree-filled Cales Dale. The pretty little wood avens was in flower by the side of the steep steps which carried me up and out of the valley. I left the nature reserve by way of a traditional stone stile, consisting of large slabs protruding from the dry stone wall, and followed the footpath across the fields. The views to the north were fantastic – across the tree-tops of Cales Dale, right across Lathkill Dale with its great limestone crags or scars, and on to the plateau around Haddon Grove.

The White Peak is sheep country, and the hill tops all carry rich grazing pastures. The plant life of the heavily grazed pasture is, of course, much less varied than that down in the dale, and, apart from a few spear thistles and creeping thistles and the occasional patch of stinging nettle, virtually all I saw in these pastures was grass. The turf was closely cropped in most places, but the flowering spikes of meadow grass were quite prominent, sticking up like miniature Christmas trees. Equally prominent in some fields were the spikes of crested dog's-tail, which are one-sided and reminiscent of tiny tooth brushes.

I was the centre of attraction as I walked across the field, with hundreds of sheep

Unaffected by the stinging hairs which make the nettle so unpleasant for us, families of small tortoiseshell butterfly caterpillars feed voraciously on the leaves. The families break up as the cater—pillars reach maturity and seek pupation sites.

watching my every move. The ewes had recently been shorn and their lean bodies contrasted strongly with the plump, woolly lambs. The ewes were mules, or grey-faces, reared in the north of England by crossing Swaledale ewes with Blue Leicester rams. The mules have attractive white and grey faces and they combine the hardiness of the Swaledale with the size and mothering ability of the Leicester. The sturdy black-faced lambs running with them were the result of mating the mules with Suffolk rams. Well-mothered by the mules, these lambs grow quickly and yield good carcases for the butcher.

The footpath passes through Calling Low Farm, and continues in a south-easterly direction. One of the fields was being put up for hay and contained a high proportion of red and white clover – in full flower and emitting a delightful scent. Turning left at the road, I walked between banks of meadow cranesbill, with pale walls of limestone behind them. Questions flooded into my mind: how many miles of such walls are there in the Peak District; how many stones were used to build them; how many men were employed; and how long did they take? Impossible to answer, of course, and quite pointless, so I gave up and contented myself with the remarkable scenery.

I took the footpath on the left and headed for Over Haddon by way of another hayfield. Skylarks trilled above me and the land fell away in front as it dropped down towards Lathkill Dale. The network of limestone walls seemed to wriggle over the green landscape as if cutting it up into an enormous jig-saw puzzle. It was easy to see why this area is called the White Peak, for the walls looked almost white in the bright sunshine. The whole area contrasted strongly with the millstone grit scenery of the Dark Peak, which I could just make out away to the east on the other side of the River Wye.

The footpath eventually led me through the farmyard at Meadow Place Grange.

Beyond the farm it begins its final descent into Lathkill Dale, winding down the steep slope with a larch plantation on one side and the columnar trunks of wych elms on the other. Rosebay willowherb was in full flower under the elms, together with large clumps of male fern, and tufted hair grass whose leaves and stems were full of cuckoo-spit, in which the nymphal froghoppers were nearly mature. At the bottom of the slope the path crosses the river by means of an ancient slab bridge, consisting of large limestone slabs laid over a number of small stone pillars. The river is very shallow at this point – in fact, there is often no water at all during the summer – and this has obviously been a crossing point for man and his livestock for many centuries. Standing on the bridge, I tried to imagine what things might have looked like back in the middle of the nineteenth century, when lead-mining was in full swing: pack-horses would have been crossing the river with their loads of ore, and there would have been a good deal of activity around the mines, accompanied by a considerable noise when the steam engine was working. But, away from the immediate vicinity of the mines, the dale and the river probably looked much as they do now. As I walked back to the car park, my thoughts turned to the future. Will our descendants be able to enjoy a quiet walk in Lathkill Dale in the twenty-first century? I hope so.

Summer
AUGUST
Dentdale, Cumbria

Dentdale is a small and secluded valley situated on the western edge of the Yorkshire Dales National Park, but now officially in the county of Cumbria. Its scenery and history combine to make it one of the most interesting of the Pennine valleys. The River Dee, fed by numerous tributary becks and gills, flows westwards through the dale on a bed of hard Mountain Limestone, while the hills rising steeply on each side are built of the slightly younger Yoredale rocks. These consist of alternating bands of hard limestone, soft shales, hard sandstone, and occasional thin seams of coal. Differential weathering of the hard and soft beds produces terraces on the hillsides, although these are less obvious in Dentdale than in some of the other dales. Some of the Yoredale limestone is very dark and full of corals and other fossils. It takes a high polish and, under the name of Dent Marble, it was in great demand for chimney pieces and other ornamental uses until the end of the nineteenth century. Quarrying of Dent Marble ceased in 1900, when imported Italian marble became cheaper. Dentdale also has numerous lime kilns, where the greyer limestones were burned to provide agricultural lime for improving the pastures.

The Norsemen settled Dentdale from the west during the ninth and tenth centuries, and their influence is still very obvious, with small farms scattered throughout the dale. The Norsemen found no need to congregate into villages, and today's farmsteads occupy their original isolated positions. Rich hay meadows and grazing pastures now clothe the lower slopes of this fertile valley and support an important dairy industry; while sheep, mostly of the hardy Swaledale breed, roam freely over the higher fells. With abundant footpaths and bridleways, the dale is excellent walking country for anyone prepared to tackle moderately steep slopes and a certain amount of rough and wet ground. Woodlands, streams, meadows, and moorlands are all accessible and all abound with wildlife.

The walk described here begins and ends in the lovely village of Dent – known locally as Dent Town – which is a purely British settlement owing nothing to the Angles or to any other settlers. It is the birthplace of the eminent nineteenth-century geologist Adam Sedgwick, and it would be nice to think that the fascinating

90

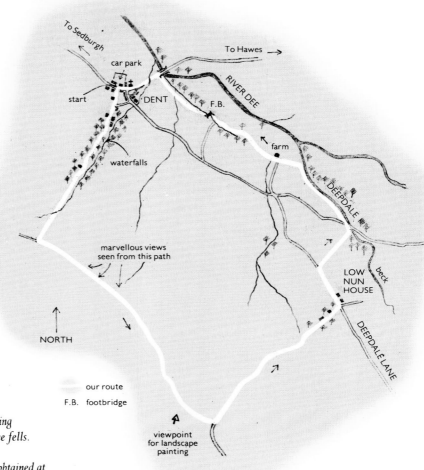

To Sedburgh

To Hawes →

car park

start

DENT

RIVER DEE

F.B.

farm

waterfalls

DEEPDALE

marvellous views
seen from this path

NORTH

LOW
NUN
HOUSE

beck

DEEPDALE LANE

our route

F.B.   footbridge

viewpoint
for landscape
painting

*The walk is a little over
4½ miles long. It begins
with a steep climb of
about half a mile, but
after that the route is quite
easy — a gently undulating track
along the hillside, followed
by a descent into Deepdale
and a virtually flat return to
Dent by way of the river banks.
Strong, waterproof footwear
is essential, for the path is rocky
in places and extremely muddy
in others. Warm clothing is
also essential, even if the sun is shining
at the start, for it can be chilly on the fells.
Morning or afternoon.*

*Excellent food and drink can be obtained at
the end of your walk at the Sun Inn in Dent
and there are also teashops in the village.*

*There is a large car park on the west side of the village.
(Map Ref: SD 704872)*

*Overleaf: Looking north across Dentdale to the lower slopes
of Rise Hill, clothed with rich sheep pasture.*

scenery of Dentdale nurtured an early interest in geology in young Adam; but in fact
he became a parson first, and when appointed Woodwardian Professor of Geology at
Cambridge he remarked that until then he had never turned a stone!

Flintergill tumbles down the steep hillside into
Dent Town by way of a long, stair-like flight of waterfalls. With care,
it is possible to walk over the slippery rocks
and to examine the alternating succession of hard and soft beds
— some of them rich in fossils — which make up this
part of the Dales and which are responsible for the stair-like
falls. The spray-filled atmosphere around the falls
supports an abundant vegetation, including wild gooseberry bushes.

My route first took me up the narrow road opposite the car park on the west side of the village, passing the village green where jackdaws were cavorting for no apparent reason and pied wagtails indulged in the serious business of catching flies. The road rises steeply past attractive white-painted cottages and is soon hemmed in between the dry stone walls typical of the Pennines. The stones are covered with lichens and mosses, and ferns sprout from the crevices, but the most conspicuous plant on these walls in August is herb robert, whose leaves were fast taking on a blood-red colour.

The tarmac soon gave way to a rough track, and I stopped here to look back over the roof-tops of Dent and across the dale to the steep slopes of Rise Hill to the north. My attention was immediately caught by the sharp division between the improved pastures on the lower slopes and the rough moorland above. The bright greens of the meadows, which have been treated with lime over the centuries to encourage the nutritious grasses, contrasted strongly in the morning light with the olive green and brown of the moorland. Some of the higher grazing pastures are being run down, however, and I could clearly see the rushes spreading over them through lack of grazing. The other prominent feature was the stone walls rising to the summit in dead straight lines. Built round about 1859, somewhat later than most other enclosures in the dales, these walls have never played a significant role as boundaries. Much more important was their role in providing work for the local population. A hard day's work might have seen six or seven yards of wall completed and a maximum of three shillings in wages. By contrast, it now costs more than £5 to repair just a yard of wall — a point worth remembering next time you are tempted to take a short cut over one.

The track rises even more steeply when it leaves the houses behind, and the sound of running water — never very far away in the dales — gets louder. Flintergill runs close to the track here, and a short detour to the left brought me to a fine cascade of waterfalls among the trees. The alternating bands of hard and soft rock are beautifully exposed here, with the nearest part of the stream running on a gently sloping bed of limestone. Carefully picking my way over the slippery rock, I moved upstream to where the slope is much steeper. Here the water tumbles over the soft shales and is rapidly eroding them. They are so soft that I could crumble pieces in my fingers, but the fossils in them are harder and I quickly found several brachiopod shells standing out from the eroded surface. Large blocks of sandstone which once formed a protective lip over the shales lie scattered over the stream bed, while higher up the stream appears to be running down a staircase as it cuts through the successive beds of hard and soft rock. It seemed just the place for a dipper, and I was not disappointed: a flash of white caught my eye, and there was the bird sitting on a boulder just below one of the falls. It bobbed up and down for a few seconds, as if proving its identity for me, and then calmly walked into the water in search of food. Dippers may spend as much as two hours a day under water, diving up to 1600 times and either walking or swimming as they hunt for small animals on the stream bed.

Moving back to the track, I was left in no doubt that the crane-fly season had started. Dozens of these leggy insects flew up as I walked through the grass. Although disliked by many people because of their spidery appearance, the adult flies are quite harmless. It is their grubs – the notorious leatherjackets – that do harm by eating the roots of cereals and other crops. The track is like a rough stream bed in places, but the grassy knolls along the sides provide plenty of resting places. They are studded with the bright yellow flowers of tormentil in August, and also with the stiff, purple spikes of betony – 'a precious herb' according to Culpeper and one which was regularly used to cure headaches. The very similar hedge woundwort also grows by the side of the track, but it can be distinguished by its more pointed leaves and greater stature, as well as by the white blotches on the flowers. Other flowers on the grassy banks include the dandelion-like autumn hawkbit and the burnet saxifrage. The latter is a delicate, white-flowered umbellifer and a good indicator of limestone soils. Few plants can survive on the rough track itself, although greater plantain and rye grass manage to thrive here because they are not damaged by trampling.

Beyond some oaks, whose fantastic root forms have been exposed by erosion of the bank, the turf was dotted with more yellow – larger splashes this time – and my thoughts turned to the supper table, for here was a fine crop of chanterelles, edible fungi of the highest quality. Their funnel shape and faint apricot smell confirmed the identification and I made a mental note to return with a basket.

A derelict barn on the right provided an excuse for a rest from the climb and also a lesson in building techniques: I could clearly see how the large and small sandstone blocks had been fitted together to form the walls. Recesses that had once held the ends of joists or rafters now held birds' nests in various stages of decay. These holes would have attracted several kinds of birds, including redstarts and flycatchers, but I think a family of robins had been the most recent tenants. A young robin, just getting its red breast feathers, watched me from the wych elm growing in a corner of the ruin. Part of the barn still has a roof and swallows were swooping in and out: no doubt they had a nest there and were rearing their second or even their third brood. There were enough flies rising from the surrounding cow-pats to feed an army of swallows.

More waterfalls on the left give further opportunity to study the Yoredale succession, although the falls are partly screened by trees. The route has been wooded right from the edge of the village, but the track now emerges from

painted lady butterfly

the trees into an area of short turf grazed by sheep and rabbits. Where limestone is close to the surface, the turf carries wild thyme and fairy flax. The dainty white flowers of eyebright are also common, while spear thistles, wisely ignored by the grazing animals, spring up close to the stone walls.

The walls were my constant companions in this middle section of the walk, bounding the grassy track on each side – reassuring if the mist should roll down from the fells. They are built with both limestone and sandstone, but it is not always easy to distinguish one from the other because lichens cover most of the stones. Where lichen growth is not too dense, fossils often show up clearly in the limestone. They include corals and brachiopods, or lamp shells, but the most abundant and conspicuous fossils are the crinoids, or sea lilies. Despite their name, these are fossilized animals; and they have been likened to many-armed starfishes borne on long stalks. These stalks in fact consist of numerous limestone discs joined together like piles of shirt buttons. They are so numerous in some areas that the rocks consist of little else and are called crinoidal limestones. The broken stalks and separated discs lie in all directions and produce beautiful patterns on a polished surface.

Soon after leaving the trees, the track begins to flatten out and there are superb views of the fells of Barbondale and lower Dentdale away to the right. Flintergill still runs to the left, and all around are small becks carving their way through the soft shales which make up most of the land surface at this point. Rushes of several kinds

Frogs revel in the damp streamside vegetation all over Dentdale, striking a variety of amusing poses while perching on wet stones and waiting for slugs or insects to present themselves.

revel in the damp soil of the gullies. The track soon meets the Occupation Road, or Okky Road, to give it its local nick-name — a broad, grassy path joining Barbondale and Deepdale. Despite its name, it is not a true occupation road at all, but an ancient fell road long used by trains of pack-horses and still carrying certain vehicular rights. (The true occupation roads were created at the time of the enclosures to allow the occupying farmers to reach their land through their neighbours' holdings.)

I turned left and the path took me across Flintergill. As I watched the stream babbling merrily over ledges and boulders, a harsh *tak-tak-tak* reached my ears. It seemed to be coming from under the wooden bridge, and then the vocalist emerged — a black bird with a white bib. It was a ring ouzel, a characteristic species of the moorland in summer, and it began to examine the streamside boulders in a very methodical fashion, pecking at them regularly and clearly enjoying itself. I suspect that it was gathering caddis flies — there were plenty resting on the walls — and stocking up with fuel for its forthcoming migration to the Mediterranean.

The Occupation Road runs more or less straight along an outcrop of sandstone — one of the few which are thick enough to show up on the geological map of the area. The sides of the track are clothed with various acid-loving grasses, hair moss, and bog moss (*Sphagnum*). Peat shows through here and there, and there are small patches of heather. Bilberries grow close to the walls, but they had been well grazed by sheep and rabbits and I found no fruits to enjoy. Marsh thistles, both purple and white flowered forms, grow in the damper patches and, considering the indifferent weather that had descended upon the fell, I was surprised to see them being visited by several freshly-emerged painted lady butterflies. This beautiful migrant, one of the world's most widely distributed butterflies, comes to us from North Africa in late spring and rears a new generation on thistles during the summer. Some of the new insects fly south in autumn and a few may actually get back to Africa, but most are doomed to die here without descendants.

The Occupation Road affords spectacular views across Dentdale and Deepdale, with streams showing up here and there like silver ribbons. The clearly defined U-shape of Dentdale indicates that the valley was originally gouged out by a glacier. Rise Hill, lightly dissected by numerous gills, has a smooth, whale-back outline which contrasts strongly with the much harder and more rugged Howgill Fells away to the west. Nearer at hand, between Dent and Sedbergh, there are some very prominent drumlins — large mounds of boulder clay dropped by the valley glacier and moulded into shape as the ice passed over them.

Dense patches of brown bent and common bent grass occur here and there along the sides of the Occupation Road, and their delicate flower heads seem to coat the ground with a brown mist. As I walked, a more sinister grey mist began to roll down from Great Coum and Whernside on my right, but the walls were still there to guide me. I turned left at the next T-junction, just as the mist started to swirl about my head, and descended into Deepdale along a track that towards the bottom resembled a boulder-strewn stream bed. Turning left on reaching Deepdale Lane, I then took the first footpath on the right, towards the wooded banks of Deepdale Beck. The fertile valley bottom, with its drifts of meadow cranesbill and its numerous trees and hedgerows, contrasts strongly with the open hillsides and, as I began this third section of the walk, I felt that I had entered a different country — especially as the mist had rolled even further down the fell and blotted out the path on which I had walked less than an hour before. But the sun still shone brightly in the valley.

Approaching Deepdale Beck, I was aware of the unmistakable smell of the stink-horn fungus — a somewhat metallic odour. The fungi were poking up under the trees and they exhibited several stages of development. Fresh specimens had the strongest odour and their tips were clothed with an olive-green slime in which millions of tiny spores are embedded. Flies were eagerly lapping up the slime and unwittingly picking up spores for transport to new sites. Older stinkhorns, from which the slime had been removed, stood stark and white on the woodland floor. Why they have evolved such a distinctly phallic shape is a complete mystery to me. The fungi first appear as soft, egg-shaped bodies among the dead leaves, and they can actually be eaten at this stage. A better idea is to gather one or two, carry them home carefully in a polythene bag, and place them under a glass jar or bowl to watch the fast growth of the phallus as it bursts through the 'egg-shell'. Several large dryad's saddle fungi were growing on the old ash trunks on the river bank; and enchanter's nightshade, one of very few flowers with just two petals, was the most conspicuous of the flowering plants underneath the trees.

The stinkhorn fungus, here covered with flies, is not always easy to see on the woodland floor, but a fresh specimen will advertise its presence with its far-reaching and decidedly unpleasant odour.

harebell

Blue and purple are the
dominant colours among the late
summer flowers in the Dales,
although yellow composites
are plentiful in some
of the meadows.

lady's mantle

hardheads or black knapweed

betony

wood cranesbill

common eyebright

wild thyme

AUGUST   *Dentdale, Cumbria*

After crossing the road the footpath continues between the beck and the hay meadows. Numerous butterflies were dancing here in the sunshine, paying particular attention to the masses of autumn hawkbit. They included meadow browns and gatekeepers, small whites, and green-veined whites. Other flowers growing by the water included great burnet, with its dark red oval heads, giant bellflower, and sweet cicely. The flowers of the latter were over, but the long, skittle-shaped seed pods readily identified this imported umbellifer.

A hedgehog trundled along a stretch of hedgerow with us — an unusual event for the daytime, possibly indicating that all was not well with the prickly urchin.

I was glad of the yellow paint flashes that mark the route where it leaves the stream, but I would have welcomed more breathing space in some of the little gateways! Designed to keep the sheep in, some of them are no more than a foot wide. I have always thrown my old wellingtons away, believing that they had no further use, but old boots have their uses in Dentdale: their tough, flexible soles are used as hinges for the narrow wooden gates. After negotiating several of these tight-fitting apertures, I found myself walking beside the Keld, which joins forces with the Dee at Dent. Bright green patches of water starwort gleamed just under the surface, and bright blue dragonflies hawked to and fro overhead. They were males and each was patrolling its own distinct territory. As I watched, two neighbouring insects flew towards each other and met at the boundary of their two domains. There was a brief clatter of wings as they met, and then each went its own way. They would soon learn the positions of the boundaries and settle down in their own areas to await mates.

Crinoid fossils are much in evidence in the stone walls around the old ford, and especially in one old gate post. Some of the limestones have acquired a high polish through continual rubbing by cattle, and it is easy to see why they were once in great demand for ornamental purposes. I crossed the stream by way of a narrow footbridge and the huddled stone roof-tops of Dent came into view across the meadow. Soon I was at the road bridge, where a huge pile of flood debris had collected. A pied wagtail sat proudly on top of it, but did he really want me to believe that this was his nest? Even an eagle would have been proud of such a pile. A few more minutes, and I was entering the quaint cobbled main street of Dent and passing the block of Shap Granite that marks Sedgwick's birthplace. The local hostelry beckoned and I finished my walk with a well-earned drink (or two), forgetting all about the chanterelles.

rowan

Bright orange fruits decorated most of the rowan
trees at the time of our walk — not a sign of a hard
winter to come, but actually an indication that
the previous year's summer had been good and conducive
to bud-formation and that the spring just gone
had produced plenty of pollinating insects.
The giant bellflower was the most prominent
flower in most of the hedgerows in the dale bottom.

giant bellflower

*sweet cicely
fruiting heads*

Autumn
SEPTEMBER
Kilndown Woods, Kent

K ent's orchards, which made it 'the Garden of England', now cover a smaller area than they did a few years ago, but vast stretches of the county are still devoted to apples, pears, plums, and cherries. Raspberries and strawberries are also important crops, as well, of course, as the famous hops. But Kent could easily be called England's garden without its fruit-growing industry, for its pleasant climate and fertile soils support an extremely rich wild flora: and what better time to explore the countryside and see these plants than September, when the hedgerow harvest is ready to be gathered and the trees are showing the first traces of their autumn colours?

The walk described here is based on the little village of Kilndown, close to the Sussex border and on the western edge of the main fruit-growing area. Right in the centre of the Weald, this is undulating country overlying the sandstones and clays of the Wealden Series. Most of the area lies on the Tunbridge Wells Sand, but patches of the slightly older and much softer Wadhurst Clay occur here and there. The whole region is dissected by narrow streams. This part of the Weald once supported an important iron industry based on ore extracted from the Wadhurst Clay, and the name Kilndown indicates that smelting went on right here. The furnaces were fired with wood from the surrounding forests. Much of the forest cover has now given way to hop fields and arable land, but there is still enough woodland left to give the countryside a natural and inviting charm.

The autumn mists were beginning to clear as I left Kilndown by way of the footpath opposite The Globe and Rainbow and headed towards Lamberhurst, and a watery sun gave promise of a fine day ahead. But I was not to see the sun again for a while, for I was soon in a dense thicket of sweet chestnut trees, readily identifiable by their long, toothed leaves. This species is a native of the Mediterranean region and was brought to Britain by the Romans. It now grows in many parts of our islands, but thrives best on the sands of the Weald. Good fruit crops are obtained in some years, but the Kilndown trees are not grown for their nuts: each tree has several trunks, or poles, springing from ground level, indicating that they are part of a coppice system grown for timber. Sweet chestnut wood is strong and durable

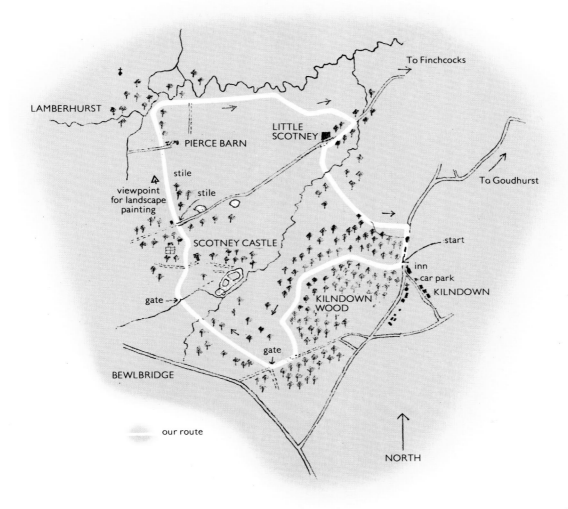

To Finchcocks

LAMBERHURST

LITTLE
SCOTNEY

PIERCE BARN

To Goudhurst

stile

viewpoint
for landscape
painting

stile

start

SCOTNEY CASTLE

inn

car park

KILNDOWN

gate →

KILNDOWN
WOOD

gate

BEWLBRIDGE

our route

NORTH

The walk is about 4½ miles long and very easy-going, with no steep climbs or descents. The path can be rather wet and slippery in places, however, and stout walking shoes with plenty of grip are strongly recommended.

Good food and drink can be obtained at The Globe and Rainbow in Kilndown during licensing hours.

Cars may be parked (tidily please) on the roadside in the village. (Map Ref: TQ 700353)

Overleaf: Lamberhurst Church, viewed across the Teise Valley from the footpath just above Pierce Barn. The fields are used for grazing, for cereal crops, and for hay. Pasture grasses and hay crops are often sown with cereals, but do not then develop fully until the cereals are harvested. The fields in the middle distance have recently been harvested and the grasses have not yet formed a complete carpet. Hops are grown in the more sheltered parts, often with high hedges or tree lines to protect them.

CALVATIA
EXCIPULIFORME

A fantastic array of toadstools and other fungi
can be found in the woods and fields of the Weald
in September, especially after a spell of wet
weather. Most of the species illustrated here were
found on or near the path through Kilndown Woods.

RUSSULA FRAGILIS:
*a fungus with
a distinctly peppery taste*

CLITOCYBE
INFUNDIBULIFORMIS

and is used mainly for fencing. The trees are cut to ground level every few years and the poles are split to produce the more or less triangular stakes known as chestnut palings, which are wired together to form a cheap but durable fence. The tree stumps soon send up new shoots, which can be cut again for palings in about twelve years. One section of the coppice is normally cut each year, so the woodland contains trees of several different ages. Some larger poles are used to support the wires in the hop fields, but sweet chestnut is not suitable for building purposes because the thicker pieces tend to crack.

A wet summer had encouraged fungal growth in the leaf litter and resulted in a tremendous toadstool crop in the woodland. I found no less than forty-seven kinds of fungi during my walk, and if I had left the path more often I would undoubtedly have found many more.

a species of HYGROPHORUS, *found in the meadow on the way to Scotney Castle*

AURICULARIA MESENTERIC

CALOCERA VISCOSA

LYCOPERDON PERLATUM

THELEPHORA TERRESTRIS

The most obvious species was *Russula emetica*, whose bright red caps were pushing up everywhere in the mixed woodland beyond the chestnut coppice. As my eyes became used to the gloom, I was able to pick out several less colourful species, including *Russula atropurpurea*, with a purple cap, and the completely purple amethyst deceiver (*Laccaria amethystina*).

A clearing around a large beech tree had been used at some time for stripping the bark from the chestnut palings, and the piles of bark had rotted down to make a rich compost. Several fungi were growing on this, including some striking clumps of the puffball *Calvatia excipuliforme*, which has a long stalk and is shaped like an old-fashioned pestle. It is edible in its early stages, while still white and clothed with its spiny warts, but the inner tissues turn dry and powdery as the spores mature. The outer layer of the head eventually breaks away and releases the spores by the million. The stalk becomes brown and spongy and is quite resistant to decay. Several of the previous year's stalks were lying around the clearing. Another puffball was also growing in the leaf litter. It was *Lycoperdon perlatum* – browner and more pear-shaped than the previous species and opening by a single pore at the top. Leaves or even rain drops falling on to the mature puffball cause clouds of spores to be pumped out just like puffs of smoke. But most of these puffballs failed to release any spores, for when I returned the

speckled wood butterfly

following day almost all had been kicked over and trodden on by some children. I have witnessed such behaviour on many occasions and have often puzzled over it. I suppose we are all taught as youngsters that toadstools are poisonous, and even evil, and destruction of the toadstools is then a logical, if misguided consequence. But it is sad that so many children seem actually to derive pleasure from kicking a toadstool to pieces. I am equally saddened to see flowers wantonly beheaded with sticks. One cannot expect every child to have a real interest in wildlife, but it would be nice to see the youngsters having a little more respect for their surroundings. They are the ones who will have to look after our countryside one day.

The path drops quite steeply beyond the clearing and opens out into a broad ride with pines on one side and more chestnut coppice on the other. Goldcrests were piping noisily as they scampered through the chestnuts, while a willow tit sang from the pines. Clusters of large, spiky fruits hung thickly from the chestnuts, but a look inside the prickly cases showed that the nuts were poorly developed: this was not to be a chestnut year. The heather fringing the ride glittered with hundreds of dew-spangled hammock-webs, each the work of a small spider which could usually be seen hanging upside-down beneath its platform. The hammock, supported by a network of silken threads, is designed to catch small jumping insects: they bump into the supporting threads and fall on to the web, and the spider scurries along to grab them before they can find their feet.

The reddish-brown toadstool *Laccaria laccata* was abundant along the ride, blending nicely with the fresh green shoots of the heather. Earthballs (*Scleroderma citrinum*) were also very numerous, sitting tightly on the ground like deformed, yellowish golf balls. They are related to the puffballs, but their spores escape through irregular cracks on the surface. The blusher was another common toadstool on this sandy ride. It is a relative of the death-cap and the fly agaric, although it has no cup at the base of its stalk, and it gets its name because the pale flesh blushes strongly when broken. The cap is pale reddish-brown with lighter patches, while the base is slightly swollen and bears a few circular ridges. This fungus first appears as a tiny mottled ball at ground level and it could easily be mistaken for an earth-ball, but close examination shows that the ball, which later expands to form the cap, always sits on a little platform formed by the swollen base of the stalk.

At the bottom of the slope, where the path turns sharp left, grew some of the largest *Boletus edulis* that I have ever seen. This is one of the most delicious of the edible fungi, with a brown cap looking like a currant bun before it flattens out. Growing under a large oak, one of these fungi must have been almost thirty centimetres across the cap, although part of it had been eaten − probably by a squirrel. The *Boletus* species differ from most other toadstools in having sponge-like pores under the cap instead of radiating gills. Many of the species are good to eat: but do make absolutely certain of your identification before you start munching!

Few butterflies are in evidence at the end of September, but a number of speckled woods were enjoying their last few days of life, flitting lazily from one sunny spot to another on their tattered wings. Flowers are also nearly over at this time of year, but the devil's-bit scabious was still plentiful at the edge of the path and it was being visited by many brown bumble bees of the species *Bombus pascuorum*. Most of these were freshly-mated queens stocking up with nectar before going into hibernation, but there were also several workers. This species has a longer season than other bumble bees and the workers could still have been feeding youngsters in their nests. Alternatively, they could simply have been enjoying the nectar feast after the break-up of their colonies. The workers were all doomed to die with the first frosts, but one very nearly died right in front of me: it flew into the web of a huge female garden spider and became firmly entangled. The spider rushed out to attack, but then discreetly changed its mind and cut the struggling bee free.

Oaks become more numerous in the mature woodland further along the path, and several squirrel dreys were noticeable in the tree tops. Hazel nuts ripening in the

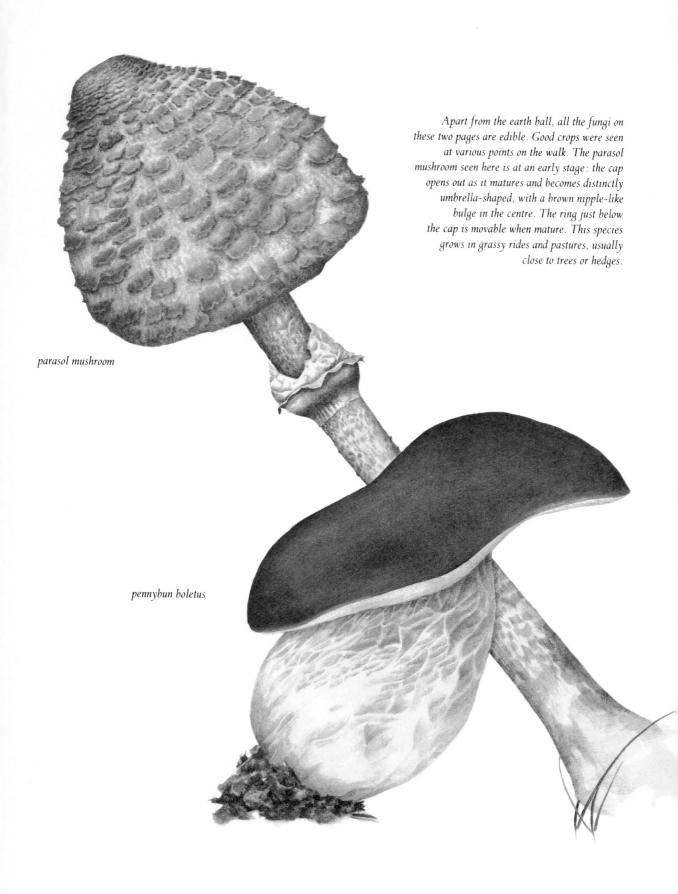

Apart from the earth ball, all the fungi on these two pages are edible. Good crops were seen at various points on the walk. The parasol mushroom seen here is at an early stage: the cap opens out as it matures and becomes distinctly umbrella-shaped, with a brown nipple-like bulge in the centre. The ring just below the cap is movable when mature. This species grows in grassy rides and pastures, usually close to trees or hedges.

parasol mushroom

pennybun boletus

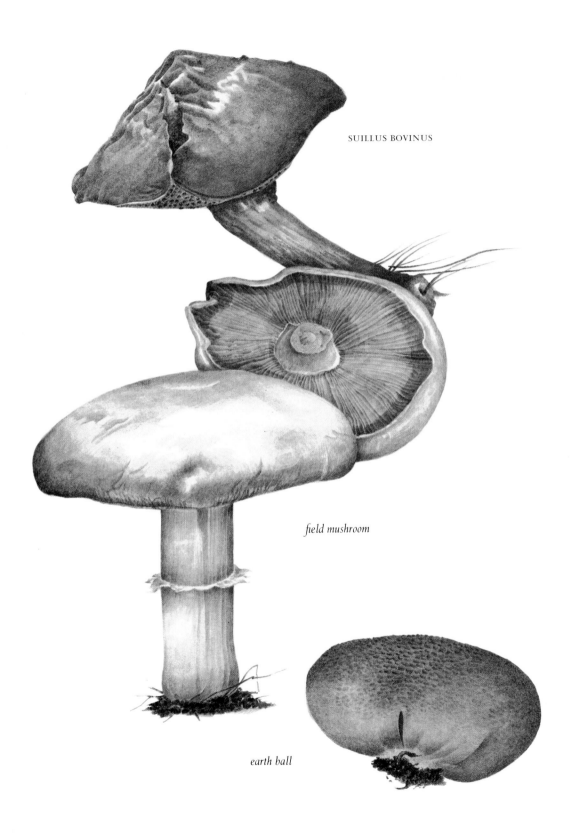

SUILLUS BOVINUS

field mushroom

earth ball

shrub layer are a great attraction for the squirrels at this time of year, and also for the nuthatches. The latter collect the nuts and wedge them into bark crevices – usually on oak trunks. They then hammer away with their beaks until the nuts split open. The kernels are removed, but the shells, usually with jagged openings, are left behind in the bark as evidence. I could hear hammering all around me as I walked along the path, but the birds remained out of sight and a quick search of the tree trunks by the track revealed only a single nutshell: the nutting season was clearly only just starting.

Rosebay willowherb was fruiting vigorously along the edges of the path, although the upper parts of the stems still carried flowers. Clouds of the tiny, fluffy seeds were blowing about in the breeze and showing very clearly how this invasive plant manages to spring up so abundantly on any patch of cleared ground. It grows particularly well on ground that has been subjected to fire – hence its alternative name of fireweed – but any cleared area will suit it. The path gradually rises again beyond the oaks and skirts another piece of chestnut coppice. I turned right at the T-junction at the top of the slope and noticed several clumps of common centaury, ragwort, and marsh thistle before entering the shade of a mixed oak and chestnut wood.

Turning right again at the next junction, still following the signposts for Lamberhurst, I soon emerged from the wood and found myself in a tree-dotted meadow which drops steeply down towards the River Bewl. Wadhurst Clay reaches the surface in this area and the ground is very damp. Fungi abound in the turf, the most conspicuous being *Hygrophorus conicus*, with its very conical orange cap, and the bright yellow *H. obrusseus.* Many fine native and exotic trees have been planted in the meadow, but some are now past their prime and several carry extensive shelves of bracket fungi – a sure sign of age and infirmity.

The bridge over the Bewl was guarded by a vociferous robin who was clearly determined to establish his territory as early as possible. No other male robin would be allowed into his domain until the next year's breeding season was over. He was still singing as I made my way up the hill towards Scotney Castle and back on to the sandstone. A tour of the castle gardens, owned by the National Trust, is a delight for anyone interested in rock gardens and colourful shrubs, but our route skirts the gardens and enters the narrow lane at the back of the castle. Turning left here, I reached another tree-dotted meadow and made for the clump of horse chestnuts and the stile at the top of the slope. Once beyond it I had a panoramic view across the valley of the Teise which clearly revealed the undulating nature of the Weald. Lamberhurst Church stands out proudly behind the attractive greens and fairways of the golf course.

Along the path descending towards the Teise, the hedgerow flagrantly displayed all the fruitfulness of September. I dined well on large juicy blackberries, taking care not to disturb the wasps which were also enjoying the feast, and admired the other

*We were never far from a robin on any of
the walks described in this book. Apart from a
few weeks in the summer, robins are strictly
territorial, each laying claim to an estate and
defending it against neighbouring robins, and our
walks took us through a succession of such territories.*

The hedgerows were full of wild fruits which were enjoyed by birds and insects alike. Blackberries also provided our own lunch during the walk.

black bryony

rosehips

blackberry

hops

fruits that made up the colourful array. The shiny red berries of the black bryony were especially noticeable, and so were the rose hips, ranging from orange to deep scarlet. Several of the rose bushes carried fluffy bedeguar galls, popularly known as robins' pincushions. Each gall, which is hard and woody under its fluffy exterior, contains several small grubs which will pupate in the gall and emerge as winged insects in the spring – just in time to lay eggs in the opening buds and start the cycle all over again. The strangest thing about these little gall wasps is that males are hardly ever produced and generations of females go on laying fertile eggs without mating.

   Half way down the field an oak tree supported a dense growth of ivy which was in full flower. It was a noisy spot, for the flowers were alive with wasps – mainly new queens bloating themselves with nectar before going to sleep for the winter. As with the bumble bees that I watched earlier on my walk, only the new queens are able to survive the winter and they start new colonies in the spring. Even noisier than the wasps was a huge flock of house sparrows at the bottom of the field. The birds were

Indian balsam grows in abundance on the banks of the Teise and has a very long flowering period: the plants were still heavy with flowers at the time of our walk, but earlier flowers had produced their seed capsules and these were already exploding impatiently and throwing out their seeds at the slightest touch. Numerous garden spiders had hung their delicate orb-webs from the plants and were obviously dining well on the many insects visiting the balsam flowers.

gleaning in the stubble, but at the slightest disturbance they flew back to the hedge, and in particular to a large holly tree, where they sat quarrelling until, in twos and threes, they all went back to the field. It is only at harvest time, when there is plenty of grain in the fields, that house sparrows congregate in such large numbers. When the grain is finished, they split up and return to their nests in and around our houses, and for the rest of the year they stay in small groups close to home.

Crossing the track near Pierce Barn, I continued down to the Teise, whose banks were covered with the beautiful pink flowers of the Indian balsam, also known as policeman's helmet because of the shape of its flowers. Bumble bees completely disappeared into the flowers as they searched for nectar, but I could not identify them because all were thickly coated with white pollen. Personally, I am less than enthusiastic about the 'dry' scent of the flowers, which reminds me of the drapery department of a large store. The plant has a very efficient method of scattering its seeds, for the pods explode when ripe and fling the seeds in all directions. You can precipitate this action by squeezing the pods gently between your finger: the generic name of the plant is not *Impatiens* for nothing, and one of its close relatives is commonly known as touch-me-not.

I did not cross the river, but turned right to walk along its southern bank. The path follows the river for some distance, giving wide views of the hop fields on the other side. Many of the hop fields are established on the rich alluvial soils of the river valley. Picking had been completed by this time and the poles and wires stood bare against the sky, but 'escaped' plants were growing here and there along the river bank. One superb example was rooted on my side of the river but twined up one of the straining wires across the river as if trying to get back into the hop field. Its bunches of ripe hops were beautifully reflected in the water below.

Hop-picking is largely mechanized now and the armies of hop-pickers no longer sweep down from London in September, although there are still some families who come down for their traditional fortnight. Whereas the bunches of hops were once picked by hand, the complete stems are now cut down and fed into machines which strip the hops from them. 'More energy-guzzling machines,' I thought. Then I saw a huge clump of Japanese knotweed growing on the river bank. This vigorous perennial is a common invader of waste ground; but it was an interesting coincidence: I had just been reading of attempts to produce fuel from it!

I left the river and its balsams close to a clump of tall poplars and followed the track along the edge of another deserted hop field. Bearing left through the gate, I passed through a field of sheep and admired the attractive oast houses of Little Scotney Farm on my right. Hops are traditionally dried in these fascinating buildings, but high-capacity, oil-fired drying sheds are rapidly rendering them obsolete. Their characteristic shapes are not disappearing altogether, however, for many are being converted to homes which will continue to decorate the Wealden landscape.

Skirting another hop field, I reached the lane and turned right along an avenue of lime trees. I then turned left on to the track just past the farm and collected more free food in the form of mushrooms growing in the grass on both sides of the track. There were also several shaggy ink caps, or lawyers' wigs, sprouting from the edges of the path, but these were past their best. Many people are surprised to learn that these fungi, which often look black and most unappetizing, are edible at all, but they are actually very good if collected when young. I like them in stews and also fried with egg and bacon, but they must be collected before they go black around the edges. The whole cap eventually degenerates into an inky fluid, whose black colour is due mainly to the spores it contains. Flies are attracted to this fluid and they carry spores away with them when they leave.

At the bottom of the meadow the path crosses the Bewl again and then rises up to reach the road by way of a lightly wooded slope. Turning right at the road, I was soon back in Kilndown, where I found I was not the only one to have finished the day's work. Some hop-pickers from London had just finished the last field and were having a celebratory drink at the inn, reminiscing about past seasons and promising to gather again in twelve months for another enjoyable fortnight.

Autumn
OCTOBER
Pulpit Hill, Buckinghamshire

The Chiltern Hills richly deserve their official designation as an 'Area of Outstanding Natural Beauty'. Made of chalk, the hills stretch from the Thames at Goring to Ivinghoe Beacon, with a steep west-facing escarpment looking out over the wide expanses of the Vale of Aylesbury. Their tops are relatively flat and heavily wooded, with beech – the basis of High Wycombe's furniture industry – being the dominant species; but they are dissected by numerous dry valleys which produce some extraordinarily attractive scenery. The steeper slopes once supported extensive downland, but much of the grassland was invaded by scrub when myxomatosis killed off most of the rabbit population in the 1950s, and some has already reverted to woodland. Some grassland remains, however, and supports a wide variety of plant life, including orchids and other rarities. The animal life is correspondingly rich, and large tracts of the Chilterns – both woodland and grassland – have been made into nature reserves.

Footpaths and bridleways weave their way over the whole area, and walking is a pleasure here at any season. But autumn is the most colourful time, with each kind of tree assuming its characteristic coat of red or gold and blending into a beautiful mosaic with its neighbours. The walk described here concentrates on the woodland margin, where the colours can be seen at their best, and takes in Pulpit Hill and Whiteleaf Cross – two famous landmarks of the Chiltern escarpment just north-east of Princes Risborough. Pulpit Hill is one of the highest points on the escarpment and is itself part of a nature reserve. The remains of an Iron Age fort can be seen on its summit.

The first frosts had already touched the Chilterns, and the autumn colours were at their best as I drove along the lanes to Pulpit Hill in bright sunshine. But the colours would not last, for the leaves were falling fast as the October winds gathered strength. A carpet of crinkled beech leaves, already quite thick, crackled underfoot as I left the car and climbed the steep path into the woods. The dark, whorled leaves of

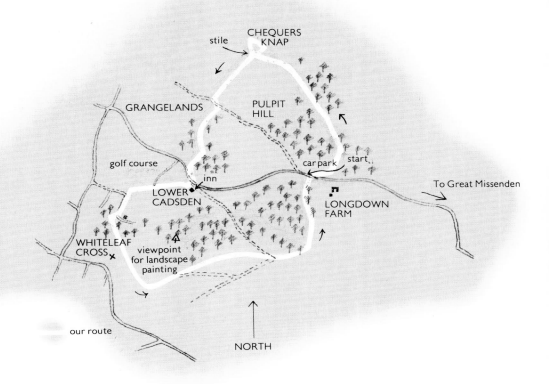

The walk is about 3½ miles long and, apart from
the initial climb and another steep haul about
half way round, it is quite easy going. Waterproof
footwear is recommended, for the woodland paths
are very wet and muddy in autumn. Footwear should also
have a good grip, for the chalk can be slippery in
damp weather.

    Begin in the morning if possible,
bearing in mind that it gets dark early in the latter
half of the month. Lunch can be taken at The Plough.
The walk can be shortened if desired by going up the
road from The Plough and straight back to the car park.

    Car park at the top of Longdown Hill on the road from
Great Missenden to Princes Risborough. Map Ref: SP 833046.

    Footpath Map No. 3 published by The Chiltern Society
at 40p will be useful.

Overleaf: The magnificent autumn colours of the beeches
and other trees in The Hangings — a large hollow in
the woodlands just to the west of Whiteleaf Cross. The
summit of Pulpit Hill can be seen through the
trees on the far right.

the woodruff showed through the golden carpet and I unwittingly gathered many of the little hooked fruits around my ankles.

A dog stinkhorn fungus stood vulgarly erect at the side of the path, and while kneeling to examine it I let my eyes wander over the surrounding leaves — a rewarding exercise, for a few feet in front of me I spotted a fine crop of earth-stars. These fungi are related to the puff-balls but they are built in a more elaborate way. The earth star is more or less spherical at first, but its fleshy outer coat soon splits into about six rays and reveals the papery inner sphere which contains the spores. The rays fold back to ground level and form the star, with the inner sphere sitting in the centre. The rays then curl under at the tips and raise the central portion above the ground so that the spores have a better chance of being blown away by the breeze. A small collar between the star and the sphere identified my earth-stars as *Geastrum*

triplex, a common species which looks very much like an onion bulb in its early stages. The pale brown stars were so well camouflaged on the mottled carpet of leaves that I doubt I would have noticed them from a standing position.

It was impossible to walk really quietly through the dead leaves, but the birds did not seem unduly worried by the noise and a goldcrest piped sweetly from a spruce branch close to my head. The sun shone strongly on my back as I passed into a small clearing and, apart from the autumn colours, it was like a summer day. The only sound as I sat there enjoying the warmth was that of a couple of blackbirds shuffling through the leaves in search of food. Clumps of the attractive purple fungus known as the amethyst deceiver decorated the ground around me, but the most striking features of this little clearing were the myriad strands of spider silk. Hanging from every branch and drifting out across the open spaces, they caught the sun's rays and shimmered as brightly as any tinsel on the Christmas tree.

Common earth-stars — freshly opened and distinctly star-like on the left, older and browner on the right with the rays curled back and holding the papery sphere above the level of the leaf litter.

Moving further up the hill, I enjoyed the strong, sweet smell of resin that was oozing from young spruce trunks. I saw a couple of small flies trapped in the sticky fluid on one tree, and my mind turned to the ancient insects that have been discovered in lumps of the fossilized resin that we call amber. Were these two flies also going to be preserved in amber, perhaps to be rediscovered on a seashore some fifty million years hence?

My route took me across another track and up to a stile, beyond which I forked right. The going became hard, not because I was still climbing but because I was on the clay-with-flint deposits which develop on most of the chalk hills. A wet autumn had left the ground waterlogged and horribly sticky. Numerous ferns were enjoying the damp conditions along the edge of the path, but very little grew in the leaf litter under the beeches. These trees cast a deep shade throughout the summer and few small plants can survive beneath them. The effect of this shading was emphasized a little way along the path, where the beeches had recently been thinned out. Bramble, rosebay willowherb, birch, and the ubiquitous sycamore saplings were growing strongly in the open areas, together with wild raspberries, now, alas,

Few small plants can survive under the shade of the Pulpit Hill beeches; but among the crunchy leaf litter of beech, hawthorn, ash, wild cherry and hornbeam we did find many toadstools, as well as the pupa shown here.

devoid of fruit. The beeches here were truly spectacular, with slim grey trunks towering seventy feet or more into the air and small rounded crowns spreading like umbrellas at the top. The straight trunks, with hardly a branch below about thirty feet, indicated that the trees had originally been packed tightly together. One dead trunk, still standing, was riddled with holes made by woodpeckers searching for beetle grubs and other insects. A loud, laughing call echoed through the woodland and confirmed the presence of a green woodpecker.

Woodpigeons clattered noisily in the tree-tops as I turned left at the T-junction under the beeches. An expanse of bracken indicated a rather more acidic soil and here, close to the edge of the wood, the beeches branch much lower down. It is noticeable that the branches are best developed on the side facing outwards, where they get the most light. I then passed into an area of younger woodland, where small beeches mingle with hawthorn, ash and field maple. The leaves of the latter were a particularly bright shade of yellow, contrasting strongly with the deep red leaves of the wild cherry, most of which had already fallen to the ground. Hornbeam is also common in this area. Its leaves might be confused with those of the beech at first, but they are more yellow than beech leaves at this time of year and quite strongly toothed. The colourful tree-lined drive leading to Chequers can be seen in the valley away to the right.

The ground is very wet on this ill-drained and heavily shaded north-facing slope and it supports large clumps of tufted hair-grass. The deep green leaves of this plant are strongly ribbed and coarse to the touch – sharp enough, in fact, to cut unwary fingers. The attractively branched flower heads are rather dainty in comparison with the bulky leaf cushions. Some that I saw still carried flowers, but most had seeded and had already been stripped of their seeds by the birds. The woodland floor was littered with twigs, many of which bore the pretty coral-spot fungus so familiar to gardeners who try to use their pea-sticks for more than a year or two. The pink spots are just the fruiting parts of the fungus, the bulk of which lives inside the twigs and quickly rots them.

The trees gradually thinned out on my right, and then began the most colourful stretch of the walk, heralded by some splendid silver birches with yellow leaves gleaming in the sunshine. The rough downland falls gently away on the right to reveal superb views of Happy Valley, a deep combe cut into the western edge of the chalk escarpment above the village of Great Kimble. The valley, part wooded and part downland, supports an extremely rich fauna and flora, including the best native box woods in Britain. Together with the surrounding grassland, it has been scheduled as a 'Site of Special Scientific Interest' and it is managed as a nature reserve by the Berkshire, Buckinghamshire and Oxfordshire Naturalists' Trust (BBONT). Controlled sheep grazing is used to maintain the open grassland and prevent further encroachment of scrub.

For a wider view of this splendid scenery, I walked a little further down the bridleway, crossed the stile on the right, and climbed to the top of Chequers Knap. The flat top of this strange, isolated knoll gives it a rather artificial appearance, but it is believed to be a natural mound, with the flattening caused by the thousands of people who have stood there to admire the view. The grassland below the Knap is studded with sycamores – which when I saw them were rapidly greying as the leaves shrivelled and showed their pale undersides before falling – and also with beeches and birches. Great Kimble church pokes up through the trees at the bottom of

Happy Valley, and beyond it the Vale of
Aylesbury stretches away into the distance.
I could just make out the town of Aylesbury
itself through the grey mist lingering
over the low ground.

Away to my right, in the direction from
which I had just come, stood more birches with
brilliant yellow leaves, and some majestic horse chestnuts
ablaze with deep orange, but my eyes kept returning
to the trees on the opposite side of Happy Valley.
The mosaic of colours was dominated by
the beeches' rich copper. Yellows were provided
by birches, maples and wych elms, while the
ashes and sycamores added greyish-greens.
Splashes of red indicated fruit-laden whitebeams.

Returning to the stile, I noticed a large clump of deadly
nightshade displaying its purplish-black berries. A chalky soil at the
woodland edge is the typical habitat for this beautiful but very
poisonous plant. The Ridgeway Path, one of Britain's long-
distance footpaths, snakes up the grassy hillside from the east and
meets the bridleway at the stile. The next part of my walk
was along this famous path.

buckthorn

*traveller's joy
or old man's beard*

The scrub-covered hillsides carry a wealth
of wild fruits in autumn. When fully
ripe, the delicate pink fruits of the
spindle split open to reveal the brilliant
orange coats of the seeds.

spindle

Whiteleaf golf course in the afternoon
sunshine, with strong shadows of the trees
creating fascinating patterns on the fairway.

Just below the Knap, the path leaves the bridleway and veers off to the left to cross another stile. Here I rested and admired some more fine views along the lower slopes of Pulpit Hill and across to the green fairways of Whiteleaf Golf Course, on which I would shortly be walking. I crossed the old rifle range, with its butts tucked into the hillside on the left, and continued along the well-worn track of the Ridgeway. The shallow soil has been worn away in many places and the bare chalk is exposed. These slopes form part of another BBONT nature reserve and their rough, scrubby grassland contrasts strongly with the dark green of the haymeadows on the right. I saw a few ragworts still in flower, but most of the colour was provided by the shrubs. Hawthorn, buckthorn, privet and dogwood were all laden with fruit, and many were also draped with the brilliant red hips of the wild rose. A few junipers and crab apples grow among the other shrubs, and above them stand several beautiful whitebeams, named for the white undersides of the leaves. In the autumn sunshine the dense clusters of red fruits flickered like flames against the brown and grey background of the leaves.

A few blackberries lingered here and there. They are supposed to belong to the Devil after the end of September, but this didn't worry the shiny bluebottles and greenbottles that were eagerly lapping up the sweet pulp. I crossed another bridleway and continued down the track through the scrub-covered field known as Grangelands. This area was under cultivation until the war, but is now part of the BBONT reserve. The colours still blazed, and for the first time I was able to see the full glory of Pulpit Hill itself. The beeches clothing the summit gleamed copper and gold, and below them the canopy was varied with assorted pale greens and the dark green of scattered yew trees. The red of the whitebeam and the yellow of the maple stood out clearly along the lower edges of the woodland. Our Iron Age ancestors certainly knew what they were doing when they built their fort on the top of Pulpit HIll, for it must have given them a commanding view right across the Vale of Aylesbury as well as over the rest of the Chilterns to the east and the south.

I continued down the slope of Grangelands, past some spindle bushes decorated with their pink and orange fruits, and soon reached the road, where I turned left and headed for The Plough. My timing had been good and lunch was being served. A plateful of tasty ploughman's pie set me up for the rest of the walk, which promised to be just as sunny as the first part. I retraced my steps for a few yards and then turned left up a narrow footpath. Traveller's-joy, with stems like tropical lianas, hung curtain-like from the tall hedge as I climbed up to the edge of the golf course. Negotiating the fairway without being hit, I stopped on the far side and turned to admire the view. Clumps of trees scattered over the course blazed yellow and gold in the afternoon sun, and their long dark shadows streaked across the bright green grass like giant tattoos. Pulpit Hill still dominated the skyline to the north, and the extent of the scrub invasion of Grangelands was clearly visible.

beech

Autumnal alchemy turns the leaves
into a rich variety of golds, reds,
and browns, completely
transforming the trees in a
matter of days.

field maple

guelder rose

Skirting the delightfully situated cricket field, I turned left by the pavilion and then right by the golf club. A footpath runs along by the reservoir on the right, but I heaved myself up the steep slope to the left and reached the top of the Chiltern escarpment, where the broad, grassy path is fringed by dense scrub. The shiny red berries of the guelder rose hung from the bushes in dense clusters.

A low fence a little further along on the right marks the top of Whiteleaf Cross, a huge cross carved into the steepest part of the escarpment above the village of Whiteleaf. It has a triangular base, about 400 feet wide at the bottom, and the cross itself, with arms spanning about 80 feet, is perched on the top. The whole thing is about 250 feet from top to bottom. It is possible that the triangular base, known as the globe, is not part of the original cross and that it has been formed by natural erosion of the chalk escarpment, aided by thousands of human feet. It has certainly been getting wider over the years, for it measured only 189 feet across the bottom in 1742. The exact age of the cross is unknown, but a description written by Francis Wise in 1742 suggests that it was then relatively new. Its purpose is also unknown.

Standing by the low fence at the top, one gets no impression of the cross, although the arms are just about discernible as hollows as one looks down the slope. For a good view of the cross, it is necessary to drop right down to the plain, from which it can be seen for miles, although the trees now obscure the lower margins. Just as the cross can be seen from a distance, so its summit affords extensive views across the Vale of Aylesbury. Tractors were busy in the fields below me, turning pale stubble into dark soil as they ploughed up and down. Some fields were already sprouting faint green lines of winter wheat or barley. Smoke rose gently from the chimneys of Princes Risborough and contributed to the afternoon haze, but I could still make out the meadows beyond the town and the dark, rounded shape of Chinnor Hill and The Cop about four miles away to the south west. It was a typical autumn afternoon, with that very characteristic but intangible atmosphere that can never be reproduced at any other season.

The sun was dropping now, but it still shone brightly on the escarpment and sent long black shadows snaking across the ground behind the beech trees as I moved into the woods. Here again the ground carries little but dead beech leaves, although a few small holly bushes manage to survive by virtue of their evergreen leaves, which can make food on mild winter days when the beeches are bare. Many toadstools thrive in the leaf litter, however, and the late-maturing *Clitocybe nebularis* was particularly common. In one area scores of these toadstools were growing in a fairy ring about fourteen yards across. They had clearly been growing there for many years, gradually spreading out from a single initial cluster.

A small wooden fence on the left marks the junction of several paths and I turned left here into the denser woodland, leaving the Ridgeway Path following the edge of the escarpment. The woodland is much used for horse-riding and is criss-crossed by numerous paths and tracks which I found rather confusing; but my aim was to keep close to the edge of the wood at first. The ground falls away on the left and I had some splendid views over the colourful beeches and other trees in The Hangings. I forked left after a little while and kept close to a barbed wire fence on my left. This brought me to a bridleway, where I turned left. I was soon back at the edge of the wood, and followed the bridleway right back to the road by the car park. The sun had set by this time and there was a distinct chill in the air. The leaves were falling even more thickly as I drove away. Soon the fiery cloak of autumn would be completely discarded.

Autumn
NOVEMBER
Dundeugh Forest, Galloway

Galloway, comprising the two counties of Wigtown and Kircudbright, is the most southerly region of Scotland. It is a land of many contrasts. The coastal areas, strongly influenced by the North Atlantic Drift, have a mild climate – there are sub-tropical gardens at Port Logan – and carry some of the most productive dairy pastures in Scotland. This is the home of the famous Galloway cattle. In marked contrast to these gentle green lowlands, the interior of the region is wild and mountainous, with several peaks over 2,500 feet. With the highest point – The Merrick – at only 2,700 feet, the Galloway Highlands lack the grandeur of the North West Highlands, but their rocky summits, numerous lochs, and extensive coniferous forests combine to form some of Britain's finest scenery. The landscapes are particularly exciting in late autumn and winter, when snow caps the highest peaks, contrasting dramatically with the dark green forests.

The forests are mainly Forestry Commission plantations, carefully planned to follow the contours wherever possible so that rather than obscuring features they actually accentuate the underlying land forms. The forests certainly enhance the scenery in most parts of the region. Most of them have been planted since 1920 – the Forestry Commission came into being in 1919 – and, although they are designed primarily to produce timber, they are important recreational areas. There is public access to most parts, and the Commission has provided numerous picnic places and forest walks, where red deer can often be seen at close quarters. The many lochs, both natural and artificial, and their surrounding grasslands are important winter feeding grounds for ducks and other birds, and there are also some interesting deciduous woodlands in the valleys. The Galloway Hills thus offer splendid opportunities to both the walker and the naturalist: and yet Galloway remains one of the least visited regions of Scotland.

The walk described on the following pages is essentially a circuit of Dundeugh Hill, a forested area set among superb scenery in the Glenkens a few miles north of the village of New Galloway. Kendoon Loch runs along the east side of the hill, and

The walk is about 5 miles long and is no more than gently undulating. It is entirely on forest roads. Normal footwear is adequate, although the roads may be muddy after rain, especially where forestry operations are being carried out.

Start in the morning or early afternoon. No refreshments are available in the immediate area.

Cars may be parked in the lay-by or by the entrance to the forest road on the A713 between New Galloway and Carsphairn. Map Ref: NX 598884. (Do not block the entrance to the forest road.)

Overleaf: Looking north from the frozen banks of Kendoon Loch to the mosaic of larches and spruces on Marscallogh Hill and the snow capped summits of the Carsphairn range in the distance.

the visitor can enjoy a wide range of landscapes in one short walk. There are also opportunities to see the Forestry Commission at work; and in this context it should be remembered that certain stretches of the walk may change considerably as areas of forest are felled and re-planted.

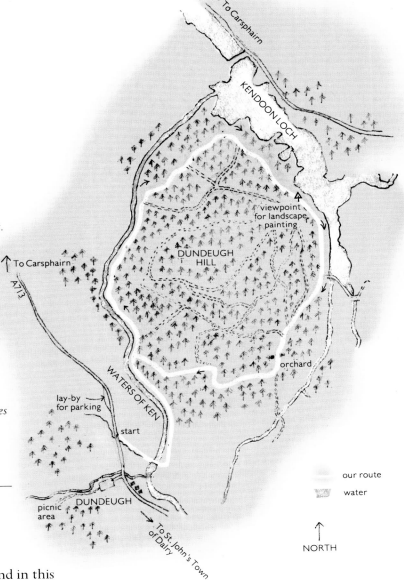

To Carsphairn

KENDOON LOCH

viewpoint for landscape painting

To Carsphairn

A713

DUNDEUGH HILL

orchard

WATERS OF KEN

lay-by for parking

start

picnic area

DUNDEUGH

To St. John's Town of Dairy

our route

water

NORTH

My drive from New Galloway to Dundeugh Hill took me alongside the Water of Ken, which, like most other rivers in the area, has been damned at intervals in connection with the region's extensive hydro-electric scheme. But the dams are generally cleverly screened by trees: they rarely intrude on the natural charm of the landscape, and the lochs blend so well with the scenery that it is easy to forget they have been artificially produced. I saw huge flocks of greylag geese grazing the riverside fields, and a group of whooper swans honked loudly as they searched for food in the frozen stubble. A herd of Highland cattle grazed contentedly on a hillside, their long shaggy coats insulating them against the icy winds blowing down from the north. But it was a sunny morning and the hillsides gleamed as the sun's rays fell on coppery bracken and the paler browns of dead grasses.

The forest road was frozen solid as I hurried along it towards the trees, and each boulder in the stream wore a collar of ice which spread out over the water like a lace doily. Felling was in progress in the forest and a strong smell of resin hung in the cold air as I crossed the bridge. The map indicates a castle on the river bank, but this former Gordon stronghold, dating from about the fifteenth century, is now nothing more than a heap of rubble covered with spruce needles and a few ferns.

I turned left soon after crossing the river and followed the forest road through the trees. Piles of logs stood by the roadside, their ends all numbered to provide information on the amount of usable timber in each piece. Most of the trees were Norway spruces, recognizable by their uniformly deep green needles and by the bluntly-pointed scales of the long cones which littered the ground beneath them. Like other spruces, they bear numerous little pegs on their older twigs. The Norway spruce was introduced from Northern Europe several centuries ago and it grows extremely well in the damp climate of western Britain. Its timber is extensively used for building and paper-making, and also in the manufacture of hardboard and similar materials. Most of our Christmas trees are also young Norway spruces.

I soon met the river again and, ignoring the turning on the right, I took the road along the river bank, with Dundeugh Hill towering steeply above me on my right. The river is fringed with oaks and birches and various other deciduous trees, including a few rowans. Their leafless, lichen-clad branches formed an attractive grey lattice against the deep blue sky, and beyond them, like the back-drop of a stage set, gleamed the snow-capped summits of the Rhinns of Kells. The plantation rising up on my right included larches as well as spruces, and there was a marked contrast between the brown, needle-covered ground under the evergreen spruce compartments and the grassy vegetation under the deciduous larches, now bare and letting in plenty of light.

Dundeugh Hill is composed largely of ancient shales and mudstones, laid down during the Ordovician Period some 450 million years ago, but the lower slopes are clothed with boulder clay and other debris dropped by the ice-age glaciers. The boulders in the river have all been washed out of these glacial deposits, and I saw many more jutting from the clay and ready to roll down the banks at the slightest provocation. As I looked at the steep roadside bank I could see the erosion of the softer deposits actively taking place. The exposed surfaces had frozen hard and large areas were covered with a delicate lattice of ice crystals. When the sun's rays reached the ice, particles started to melt and break loose, and they took small particles of soil with them as they rolled down the bank. Severe undercutting had occurred on several parts of the bank where the various forces of erosion had eaten away the lower levels and left the uppermost layer, securely bound by plant roots, as a prominent overhang. Large icicles hung from the edge like enormous crocodile teeth.

On some less steep parts of the bank I found curious patches of inverted icicles, sprouting from the ground like miniature forests. Each column of ice was about half an inch high and about the thickness of a pencil lead. Some were distinctly layered and had a satiny texture rather like that of gypsum crystals. Most of these tiny columns were capped by particles of soil, and they had obviously been forced out of the ground by the pressure of ground water in the hillside above. In the sub-zero conditions, the water had frozen in the surface layers and been pushed out of the soil pores like toothpaste. Again, as I watched, the sun's rays melted the tips of the columns, causing the soil particles to fall and to roll further down the banks.

Although some steeper banks were warmed by the radiant heat of the sun, the atmosphere remained bitterly cold and the ice on the puddles showed no sign of melting. I did not expect to see much animal life under such conditions, but there was a movement under the ice of one of the puddles, and there, in water probably less than an inch deep, swam a tiny frog. He did not have much room to move, but he was relatively safe under the insulating blanket of ice. He also had company, in the shape of a caddis larva which was laboriously dragging itself and its tubular house of sand across the bottom of the puddle.

Highland cattle can be seen
on the way to and from
Dundeugh Forest.

One of the most striking contrasts
at Dundeugh in winter is that between
the bare twigs of the deciduous
larches and the deep green
foliage of the spruces.

common larch

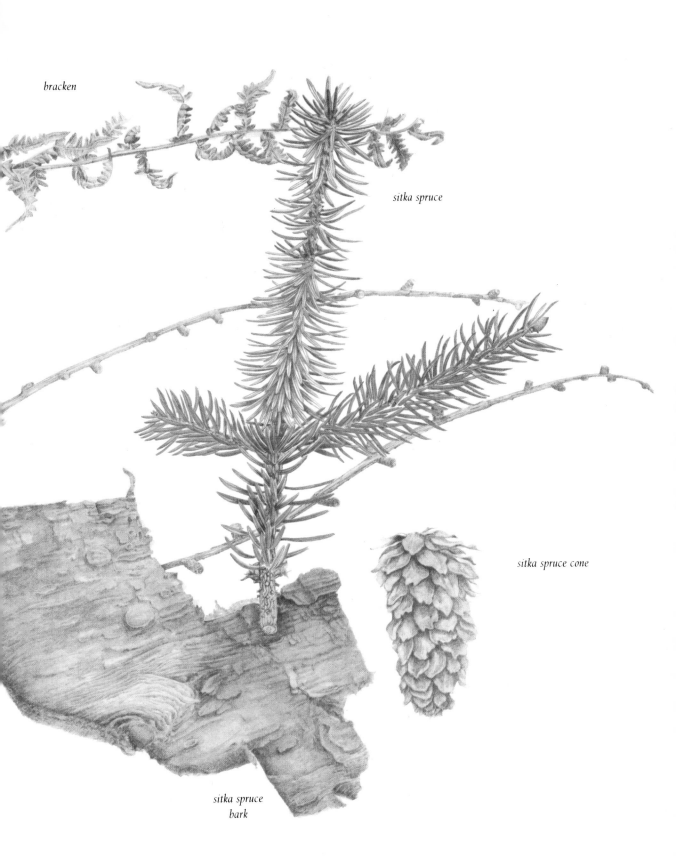

bracken

sitka spruce

sitka spruce cone

sitka spruce
bark

*Two of the fascinating
lichens growing on the exposed
hillside above Kendoon Loch.*

CLADONIA FLOERKEANA

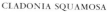

CLADONIA SQUAMOSA

The peace was broken only by the distant hum
of chain-saws as I continued along the forest road in
the sunshine. Scattered trees on the opposite hillside cast intricate
shadows over the bracken and grass. A couple of roe deer were feeding among the
trees, while some restless magpies argued over who should sit where. The deer
looked up as I approached and stared at me for several seconds before deciding not to
trust me. They bounded effortlessly away through the bracken, their white rumps
flashing a clear warning to other deer that a stranger was about.

The forest road undulates gently around the edge of the hill and eventually
makes a sharp right-hand turn. This corner stands some way above the river, and as I
reached it one of the most exciting vistas of the whole walk opened out in front of
me. Framed by dark spruces on the right and lacy grey oaks on the left, the lower
part of the picture was filled by the purplish-grey branches of the riverside birches,
partly in shadow, and by the silvery ribbons of the river itself as it flowed between the
dark boulders. Rich brown, bracken-strewn hillsides filled the middle of the picture,
while in the distance and looking more like clouds than mountains stood the snowy
summits of the Carsphairn range.

*So cold was the ground of Dundeugh Hill that
every dead leaf was coated with frost (below left) and the
scattered snow flakes retained their intricate
shapes when they landed.*

Shortly beyond this picturesque corner the road
leaves the river, and I was now hemmed in by spruces
on both sides. Rushes and large clumps of tufted hair
grass revelled in the damp, shady conditions by the side
of the road, and densely branched clumps of the
fairy club fungus *Ramaria invalii* sprouted from the thick carpet
of needles under the spruces. The road gradually climbs up out of
the valley, and the banks on the right are composed of hard
shales and mudstones instead of boulder clay. Thick carpets of moss
grow on these shady banks. A fire-break descending almost
vertically on the left afforded a dramatic, but narrow view of the
sun-drenched hillside on the other side of the river.

I was still hemmed in by spruces as I turned along the
north side of the hill, but felling had recently taken
place along the edges of the road and the spruce tops lay
scattered on the ground. Too slender to be used for
timber, these uppermost parts of the trees are frequently
sold as Christmas trees.

With the outer trees gone, the dark interiors of the forest compartments were revealed and I could clearly see the straight, tightly-packed trunks with only wispy dead branches on their lower regions. No greenery can survive in the deep shade of the interior.

Bluish-grey foliage began to appear in the forest as I approached Kendoon Loch, indicating the presence of Sitka spruce. The needles of this species have two broad bluish-white bands on the underside, and the cones are shorter than those of the Norway spruce. The cones also have very crinkly and coarsely-toothed scales. Sitka spruce is a native of North America, but it is now the most important timber tree in western Britain. It can survive in more exposed places than Norway spruce, hence its presence here on the north-facing slopes of Dundeugh Hill.

The spruces gave way to scattered Scots pines as I reached the edge of the plant-ation, and here I left the road and walked on to the exposed, bracken-clad slopes above the loch. The wind almost took my breath away, but the view was even more breath-taking. The snow-covered granitic dome of Cairnsmore of Carsphairn dominated the northern skyline, with Black Shoulder – now white – in front of it and Beninner to the right. Heavy cloud hovered over these mountains and threatened more snow: in fact, as I watched, the white shawl crept distinctly lower down Black Shoulder. But elsewhere the sky was clear and its bright blue was reflected brilliantly in the icy waters of the loch. Marscallogh Hill on the opposite side of the loch wore a patchwork coat of green and brown, produced by the mixture of Sitka spruce and leafless larches growing on its slopes.

Kendoon Loch has been created by the damming of both the Water of Ken and the Water of Deugh, and one of the two dams was clearly visible to the left of my vantage point. As I looked out over the water, seven herons rose laboriously from the valley below the dam. They just managed to clear the wall, and then they turned into the wind and immediately gained height. They turned again, and with a lazy flapping motion allowed the wind to carry them further down the loch. A cormorant streaked low over the water with a much more direct and purposeful flight.

I returned to the road and the shelter of the trees, but the respite was short-lived: the road drops down from this northern corner of the hill and I was soon walking close to the water's edge and back in the teeth of the gale. The surface of the loch was being whipped into waves, and a mixed flock of mallard and goldeneye wisely kept in the calmer water close to the opposite bank. But a cormorant – presumably the one which had flashed past me earlier – braved the cold wind and sat on a fallen branch on the most exposed part of the shore.

The clouds over the northern mountains were now very black, producing a most dramatic contrast with the snow: and they were coming my way. A few snowflakes fell around me, and the ground was so cold that they showed no sign of melting.

Dense stands of reed canary grass grow around the margins of Kendoon Loch and provide shelter for many water birds.

*Red deer live in Dundeugh Forest, but they are
not easy to observe. Much better views of
the deer can be obtained at the Deer
Park on the road from New Galloway to Newton
Stewart, although even here the deer
are extremely well camouflaged when
roaming through the dead bracken (right).*

With the aid of a lens, I was able to make out the details of their intricate and per-
fectly symmetrical patterns. The flakes were about two millimetres in diameter and
each was like a miniature flower or lace table-mat, with six branching arms. The
patterns varied from flake to flake, but the arms of any one snowflake were always
identical. It is one of the fundamental laws of nature that ice crystals have a hexagonal structure, and snowflakes are thus always six-sided. But there are infinite
variations on the basic arrangement. Some flakes are simple stars with six narrow
arms, but the arms are usually elaborately branched and decorated. In extreme cases
the spaces between the arms are completely filled to produce hexagonal discs. Perfect
symmetry is always maintained. We don't know how snowflake patterns are formed,
but it does seem that the disc-like flakes are formed at high altitudes in extremely
cold and blustery conditions. My flower-like flakes would have been formed at fairly
low altitude, probably in the black clouds drifting south from the mountains.

The sounds of the chain-saws became louder as I walked on past the loch's southern dam, and I arrived in an area which was being clear-felled. The power-saws
ripped through the nine-inch trunks in seconds, and the tractor-mounted winches
quickly dragged the felled trunks to the roadside – often pulling three or four at one
time. I watched as the trunks were rapidly sawn into lengths and stacked by the road.
The saw-marks made it difficult to count the annual rings accurately, but a rough
count showed about forty rings, so I guessed that these trees were a little over forty
years old. The forester confirmed that they had been planted as tiny saplings just
forty-two years previously. A new crop of saplings would soon be planted on this
cleared land to begin the cycle again.

The clearing was bathed in early afternoon sunshine and the coppery-brown bark
of the spruce logs glowed brightly. Their freshly-cut white ends were as dazzling as
the silver birch trunks on the far side of the clearing, but the sky behind them was
now dramatically black with cloud instead of bright blue. A kestrel also appreciated
the clearing, no doubt finding plenty of homeless voles as he hovered over the debris.

Ignoring the road going off to the right, I continued southwards until I reached a splendid Norway spruce standing guard over the ruined buildings of Dundeugh. A derelict orchard bore a fine crop of lichens, and a few apples lingered on the trees. A roe deer was enjoying the windfalls until he spotted me and made off into the forest. Bearing right beyond the orchard, I was soon back in the shade and hemmed in once more by the spruces as I followed the road around the south side of the hill. Again, the trees had been felled along the margins and I examined several slices of wood cut from the trunks. The annual rings made attractive patterns, which varied with the angles at which the trunks had been cut. The inner surfaces of the bark also bore intricate markings – the work of bark beetles which had been tunnelling in the nutritious tissues just below the surface.

It was still bitterly cold and the scattered snowflakes were still not melting. I quickened my pace in an attempt to keep warm and soon arrived back at the river bank on the west side of the hill, from where I retraced my steps to the car. There were a couple of hours of daylight left and I drove off to look at the Wild Goat Park between New Galloway and Newton Stewart. The goats, feral rather than truly wild, hurried to the fence in anticipation of food and made short work of my last two apples. I finished the day watching the red deer in the Deer Park just to the west of New Galloway.

Winter
DECEMBER
Hadrian's Wall, Northumberland

The rolling hills, or fells, of Cumbria and Northumberland were once the most northerly outposts of the Roman Empire. Since there is no effective natural boundary in this region the Emperor Hadrian ordered the construction of a great wall stretching from the Solway to the Tyne 'to separate the Romans from the barbarians'. Building began in about AD 122 and the completed wall stretched from Bowness to Wallsend. It was once known as the Picts' Wall, for it was built essentially to repel the Picts, but today it is usually called Hadrian's Wall or simply the Roman Wall. It had a chequered history during the Roman Occupation and was actually abandoned for a time when Hadrian's successor, Antoninus Pius, pushed northwards into Scotland and created a new frontier along the line of the Forth and Clyde valleys. The wall suffered large-scale damage on at least three occasions, but was rebuilt each time until it was finally abandoned at the end of the fourth century.

Although much of the wall has now disappeared through the removal of stones for house-building and enclosures, several sections remain almost intact; and the walk described here takes in just over a mile of one of the best preserved sections, to the north-east of Haltwhistle, just inside the Northumberland National Park. The scenery here is spectacular, and is dominated by the Whin Sill, a huge sheet of volcanic rock up to 200 feet thick which forms rugged, north-facing cliffs where it reaches the surface. The Roman Wall perches on top of these cliffs in several places. The other rocks of the region comprise sequences of hard limestones and sandstones and softer shales, and their differential erosion is responsible for the rolling or undulating nature of the countryside. The harder beds produce ridges, mostly running east/west and having fairly steep north-facing scarps, while the softer rocks form the lower ground.

As one would expect of an area that served as a frontier zone for more than 250 years, there is much archaeological interest here apart from the wall itself. Among the important sites are the famous Housesteads Fort and the Vindolanda Settlement a little way to the south. It was at Vindolanda that I began my walk, after driving along part of Stanegate, the Roman road from Carlisle to Corbridge.

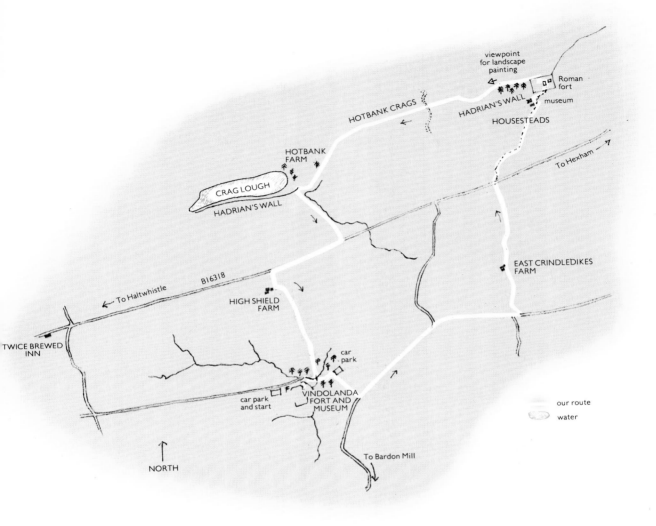

viewpoint
for landscape
painting

Roman
fort

museum

HADRIAN'S WALL

HOUSESTEADS

HOTBANK CRAGS

To Hexham

HOTBANK
FARM

CRAG LOUGH

HADRIAN'S WALL

EAST CRINDLEDIKES
FARM

B16318

← To Haltwhistle

HIGH SHIELD
FARM

TWICE BREWED
INN

car
park

VINDOLANDA
FORT AND
MUSEUM

car park
and start

our route

water

To Bardon Mill

↑
NORTH

The walk is about 5½ miles long and, although there are no really steep climbs, there are several tiring slopes. In addition, one often has to contend with strong winds in December. Waterproof footwear is obviously necessary in snowy conditions, but normal walking shoes are suitable for other times.

No refreshments are available on the walk, but The Twice Brewed Inn is conveniently situated on the B6318 just to the north-west of Vindolanda.

The Vindolanda Museum is open every day except Christmas Day.

There is a large car park on the west side of the Vindolanda site. Map Ref: NY-69664. Another can be found just to the east of Vindolanda. Map Ref: NY774665.

Overleaf: Looking west from Housesteads Crags, with Hadrian's Wall snaking its way over the snow-covered tops of Cuddy's Crags and then Hotbank Crags. Columnar blocks of the dolerite rock which forms these precipitous outcrops of the Whin Sill can be seen on the left.

My first thought on seeing Vindolanda under a light covering
of snow was that the Romans must have been mad to leave
their Mediterranean homes for the bleak, though admittedly
beautiful, fells of Northumberland. Of course, they had their
reasons – among them the important lead and silver deposits in
the rocks – and many of the people probably came from
mountainous regions where snow would have been a regular
occurrence; but life must nevertheless have been hard on this
northern frontier. Vindolanda, also known as Chesterholm,
came into being as a military fort on Stanegate some forty years
before Hadrian's Wall was built, and it later acquired a civilian
settlement. Excavations have been taking place for many years,
and in order to see what has been found I made my way
through the East Gate and down to the Vindolanda Museum
which nestles in a deep valley to the east of the site.
The museum contains a fascinating array of tools and
other objects recovered from the Vindolanda excavations.
Footwear, locks and keys, drawer handles, glass bottles,
jewellery, and some extraordinarily modern-looking
metal chains and knives reveal a great deal about the
inhabitants of the settlement and how they went about
their work. The museum also contains a reconstructed
kitchen of a typical frontier

beech twig
still bearing cups

Beech and ash trees, both easily identified
by their buds in winter, grow well in
the more sheltered places around Hadrian's
Wall, and especially in the valley
running through Vindolanda. In more exposed
places their branches are pruned by the
wind and they are carved into unusual
shapes. Spear thistles are abundant in the
pastures and along the line of the
wall itself.

ash twig

spear thistle

house, complete with baby in cradle and a warm floor covering of dried bracken.

Leaving the museum garden at the opposite end I walked up the lane, pausing frequently to admire the view of dark pines in the valley behind me, backed by the snow-covered pastures and windswept Highshield Farm on the skyline. Turning left at the T-junction, I stopped again to look back at Vindolanda. The undulating nature of the countryside is very apparent from here, with narrow tree-filled valleys snaking their way between the fields. The dead-straight Stanegate stretches away to the west. Barcombe Ridge rises sharply to the east of the road, with a lone standing stone on its crest. The hill is too steep for agriculture and the light snowfall could not conceal the dense growth of heather and bracken.

The improved pastures on the lower slopes to the west of the road carry plenty of livestock, but there is not a lot of bite for the cattle in December and the animals rely on a supplement of hay. I watched a herd run excitedly towards the gate when the daily bale arrived on the tractor, and admired the valiant efforts of some week-old calves as they struggled along with their mothers to see what all the fuss was about. Flocks of Swaledale ewes, recognizable by their dark and light grey faces, scraped the snow away in search of food. Most of the flocks had rams running with them to produce lambs in April.

I turned right at the next junction, rejoining Stanegate for a short distance before taking the track towards Crindledykes, where the windswept beeches around the house look as if their tops have been sliced off by a giant knife. The track bears right as it climbs the hill beyond the farm, and then it was my turn to feel the force of the wind as I surveyed the scene from the top of the ridge. To the east I could see Grindon Lough, standing out dark and clear among the snow-covered fields, and Stanegate disappearing over the hills on its way to Corbridge. To the north I could just make out the low grey walls of Housesteads Fort sprawling over the snowy hillside, with the Whin Sill rising up to Sewingshields Crags on the right. The fort seemed quite close, but distances are deceptive here and I had several more ridges and hollows to negotiate before I reached it. A small gap in one of the limestone ridges had been swept clear of snow by the wind, and I could see large patches of dog lichen growing in the turf. Wild thyme was also conspicuous. The grasses consisted mainly of crested dog's tail — whose pale, dead spikes still poked up through the snow — and blue moorgrass. The latter, recognizable by its abruptly-pointed blades which resemble the prows of miniature boats, is characteristic of the northern limestones.

The path is not very obvious when snow covers the fields, but I headed for the ladder-like stile at the side of the road and then made my way up the final twisting track to the fort. A flock of hardy Cheviot ewes moved politely aside as I passed, but some equally hardy blackface ewes merely stood and stared.

Tucked right up against Hadrian's Wall, Housesteads Fort was one of seventeen forts built to house the border garrisons. It was strategically placed to guard the gap

The greyish lobes of dog lichen are important constituents of the turf in the stonier parts of the pastures.

where Knag Burn flows through the ridge of the Whin Sill. One thousand soldiers once lived in the fort and, as far as can be deduced from the excavated remains, they were housed in ten long barrack rooms. The whole fort was exceedingly well-appointed, with a hospital and an elaborate drainage system.

I left the fort by the north-west corner and the next part of my walk was on the Roman Wall itself. Like the fort, the wall in this region is owned by the National Trust, and I gladly fed the collecting box to help with the excellent restoration work which the Trust is doing here and on many other nationally important sites. The first part of the wall, where it skirts the lichen-covered trees of Housesteads Wood, has been cleared of rubble and generally tidied up, but it has not been renovated and the remaining stones are just as they were laid by the Romans. Perched on the edge of the Whin Sill, with a sheer drop over Housesteads Crags on my right, I was glad that the wind was in the north and pushing me away from the edge.

Just to the west of Housesteads Wood lie the remains of Milecastle 37, one of the best-preserved of the small forts that were built every Roman mile (1620 yards) along the length of the wall. Each milecastle was large enough to house up to fifty of the men who patrolled the wall, and they were all connected by the Military Way – a narrow road running just to the south. Little of this can be seen today, but its position is marked in some places by a sheep path and some finer grasses.

To the west of the milecastle the path runs along the southern side of the wall, and I gained some relief from the north wind as well as an opportunity to examine the wall itself. Although this section has recently been renovated by the National Trust, the original Roman facing stones have been used to preserve its true appearance and the original line has been faithfully followed. The facing stones are all carefully trimmed blocks of gritstone with visible faces measuring about seven inches by eleven inches. They extend about twenty inches into the wall. The original plan was for the wall to be ten feet thick, but this was later modified and in most places it is between seven and eight feet. The width is not constant, however, and there are some prominent joins on the south face. The north face has no such joins and it seems likely that the line of this face was accurately laid down by surveyors. The

*The swampy area around Crag Lough
supports numerous small sallows, which were
still scattering their fluffy fruits
early in December — possibly resulting from a
late crop of flowers in the summer.*

numerous gangs of workmen engaged in building the wall would all have worked to this fixed line, but each gang presumably used its own discretion as to the width and this led to the irregularities on the south side. The wall was once about fifteen feet high, with a six-foot parapet on the top, but few surviving sections are more than about four feet high.

Numerous lichens grow on the stones of the wall, the most conspicuous being *Rhizocarpon geographicum*, one of the so-called map lichens. It forms bright green patches with narrow black borders, and when neighbouring patches meet the borders interlock and look just like boundaries drawn on a map. Many grasses grow on the top of the wall, together with the ubiquitous plantains and daisies. I did not expect to see many flowers here in winter, and it was quite a surprise to find the tiny white blooms of common whitlow-grass peering timidly from between the stones. The normal flowering season for this plant, which is a member of the cabbage family and not a grass at all, is between March and May. Shepherd's purse was in flower further along the wall, but this was less of a surprise because it regularly flowers throughout the year.

As I dropped down into the next hollow and then began to climb up over Cuddy's Crags, the sun came out and what had been a rather bleak landscape suddenly sparkled into life. It was an exhilarating experience, but at the same time there was a strange sense of isolation, for as I looked out over the wild and beautiful country to

A view of the walls of the Housesteads Fort, before the snow came.

Not a Roman graveyard, but part of the granary at Housesteads Fort, showing the short pillars which supported the wooden floor.

the north my only companions were the cattle quietly grazing in the rush-filled pasture far below. At that moment it was hard to imagine that this stretch of wall could ever be compared to Regent Street in the rush hour, but such comparisons have been made when thousands of visitors walk the wall in summer.

The views from Cuddy's Crags are magnificent, and it is easy to understand why this is the most popular stretch of the wall. I stood there for almost an hour, bewitched by the grandeur of the scene and by the ever-changing patterns of light and shade as superb cloud formations scudded across the sky. To the east, the skyline is dominated by Sewingshields Crags, with the wall snaking its way over the summit and Broomlee Lough glinting below it. This is a famous view, known the world over, and few visitors can resist taking photographs of it. Hunter Davies, in his excellent book *A Walk along The Wall*, described this stretch as like walking through a picture postcard.

Nearer at hand, on the steep face of Housesteads Crags just to the east of Cuddy's Crags, I could see the columnar jointing of the dark dolerite rock that forms the Whin Sill. To the north, I looked out across the rush-filled moorland pasture to Greenlee Lough, and beyond that to the dark expanses of the conifer plantations of the Wark Forest. Far to the north, I could just make out the snow-covered Cheviot Hills. The view to the south is quite different. This is good grazing land and the pastures are enclosed by networks of stone walls. Trees are confined mainly to the steep banks of the streams that carve up the undulating countryside. The scenery was probably much the same when the Romans were here, although there would have been a few more trees to the south of the wall and the northern woodlands would have consisted largely of oaks and alders instead of conifer plantations.

It was with some reluctance that I left my vantage point and continued westwards along Cuddy's Crags. A small flock of Bewick's swans flew overhead as I walked. They were heading south and no doubt taking advantage of the fine conditions to complete the final stage of their journey from the Arctic to their winter quarters in southern Britain. The wind had dropped by now and I was quite warm by the time I dropped into Rapishaw Gap on the west side of Cuddy's Crags. Here I joined the Pennine Way for the climb over Hotbank Crags and some more picture-postcard views – this time to the west. As the path drops down past Hotbank Farm into Milking Gap, the scene is dominated by Crag Lough, an attractive lake bounded on the south side by the near-vertical cliffs of the Whin Sill. Sallows, birches and other trees fringe the lake and, together with a good growth of reeds, provide good shelter for water birds. A small flock of tufted ducks displayed their diving abilities on the northern part of the lake, and as I watched from the trees on the south-eastern corner several small flocks of mallard flew in.

Retracing my steps to Milking Gap, where the wall has long since disappeared, I turned down the track alongside Bradley Burn. Water was flowing in the burn, but

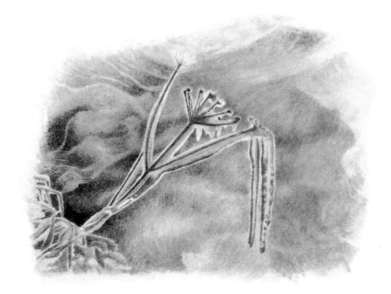

Leaning into the splash zone of Bradley Burn, a small umbellifer has become coated with ice and turned into a tinkling crystal chandelier.

its margins were a fairyland of ice: splashes of water had frozen on the vegetation and the ice had gradually built up until grasses looked like slender candles and overhanging umbellifer heads resembled the most intricate of glass chandeliers. They all tinkled sweetly in the breeze. A dipper foraged from boulder to boulder, no doubt glad of the heat-exchange system which prevents small birds from losing all their body warmth through their cold feet. A flock of fieldfares, true to their name, foraged diligently in a thistly field, probably finding a variety of seeds and small invertebrates under the snow, while a skein of geese passed overhead.

A slight hollow on the right of the track marks the position of the vallum, a deep ditch which the Romans dug some time after the wall was constructed. Running parallel to the wall and a little to the south of it, the vallum served to prevent unauthorized access to the frontier zone. I turned right along what is known as the Military Road (not to be confused with the Romans' Military Way). This was built to carry artillery between Newcastle and the west after Bonnie Prince Charlie had taken Carlisle and the north-west of England in 1745.

After reaching Highshield Farm, I followed the yellow marker posts across the gently sloping fields and back to Vindolanda. A Roman milestone still stands close to where the footpath joins Stanegate. Before leaving Vindolanda, I took a look at the full-scale replica of a section of Hadrian's Wall which has been erected on the site. The sun was disappearing fast and the wind was getting up again by this time, and as I walked around the parapet the memory of Cuddy's Crags faded just a little. I don't think I would have enjoyed being a Roman frontier guard after all — certainly not in the winter.

Winter

JANUARY

Bradwell and the Blackwater, Essex

The special quality of the light in the coastal regions of East Anglia has long been loved by artists. Although the relative purity of the air here undoubtedly helps, it is mainly due to the flatness of the land, which means that any picture or landscape has a greater proportion of sky, and therefore a brighter light, even in winter. The landscapes themselves are variable: narrow rivers thread their way through the fields in shallow, wooded valleys and gradually open out into winding estuaries and a deeply dissected coastline, especially in the south. The estuaries are popular with sailors and naturalists alike, and several bird reserves lie along the coasts. Thousands of geese, ducks and waders use the muddy creeks and saltmarshes as winter feeding grounds and refuges. Good coastal paths exist in many parts of the area.

The walk described here is based on the Blackwater Estuary – the largest in the region – and the village of Bradwell-on-Sea. This is a very flat area, mostly floored with London Clay, and its flatness is accentuated by the uniform height of most of the trees. This is a legacy from the last war, when the airfield, being one of the nearest to Germany, was used as an emergency base by returning aircraft. Most of the trees were cut down to make things easier for pilots bringing in damaged aircraft, and today's trees, nearly all of them elms, sprang up from the stumps. The area is devoted mainly to arable farming and is not scenically beautiful, but it has a great deal of natural history interest. The estuary, for example, is a well-known winter haunt of the Brent goose, which feeds in the saltmarshes and in the neighbouring fields. There is also much historical interest: a Saxon chapel and the remains of a Roman fort share the coastline with a twentieth-century nuclear power station.

It was a typical January day and grey clouds were scudding across the sky as I made my way from the car park along the well-worn track towards St Peter's Chapel. This little road was trodden by the Romans more than 1700 years ago, when they occupied the Fort of Othona and defended the coast against Saxon attacks. The fort has virtually disappeared, but more recent defences are still visible in the form of pill-boxes to the left and right of the track.

166

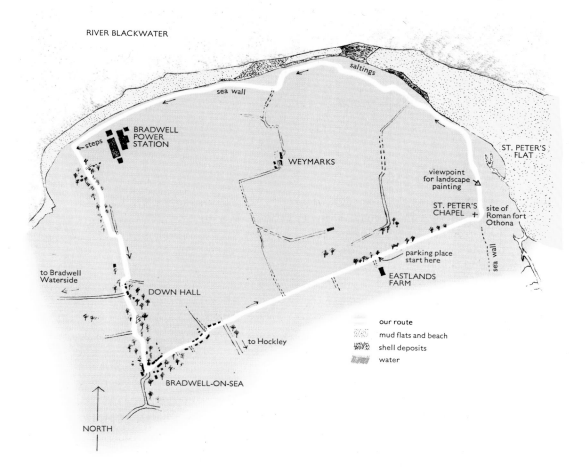

RIVER BLACKWATER

sea wall

saltings

steps

BRADWELL
POWER
STATION

WEYMARKS

ST. PETER'S
FLAT

viewpoint
for landscape
painting

ST. PETER'S
CHAPEL

site of
Roman fort
Othona

parking place
start here

to Bradwell
Waterside

DOWN HALL

sea wall

EASTLANDS
FARM

to Hockley

our route
mud flats and beach
shell deposits
water

BRADWELL-ON-SEA

NORTH

The walk is about 6½ miles long and
completely flat, but the going can be
tough in places where one has to choose
between walking on a muddy path or on
the loose sand and shingle of the beach.
Waterproof footwear is strongly
recommended.

Begin in the morning. There is a
small car park on the old Roman Road
close to St Peter's Chapel (Map Ref:
TM 025079), but the walk can equally
well be started from the centre of the
village of Bradwell-on-Sea.

Food and drink can be obtained at

The King's Head in the village and at
The Cricketers on the road to the chapel.

Overleaf: Looking south-east over St
Peter's Flat from near St Peter's Chapel:
beyond the saltings lies the North Sea,
its horizon melting imperceptibly into
the winter sky to produce an air of
mystery over the empty coastline. Despite
the heavy cloud, the saltings remain
bright and one of the many muddy creeks
can be seen cutting its way through the
Flat like a silver ribbon.

The fields, clothed with the young shoots of winter wheat and barley, sloped gently away to my right and then rose up to the sea wall like gigantic green carpets. And beyond them there was nothing: in the winter haze I could not even see where sea met sky. The sea wall stretched southwards into the mist.

Spindly elms on the left of the track showed the unmistakable signs of Dutch elm disease – falling bark and dead branches – but they were alive with bluetits searching for insects in the crevices. House sparrows huddled in the denser parts of the hedgerow, where they gained some protection from the wind. There was plenty of fresh greenery in and around the ditch, giving early promise of spring, but the dead stems of the grasses and other plants were really much more interesting. Every flower-arranger knows how attractive these dried stems can be. The grasses displayed all shades of brown, from pale buff to rich chestnut, as they rustled in the wind together with clumps of black horehound still carrying tassels of dried flowers.

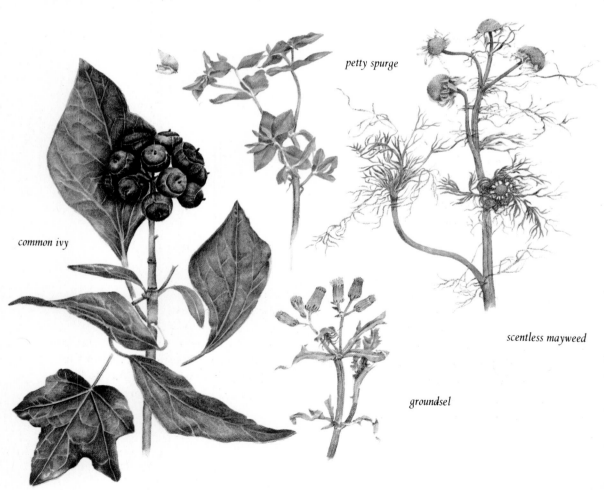

petty spurge

common ivy

scentless mayweed

groundsel

ground ivy

common field speedwell

red dead nettle

shepherd's purse

Plants can grow even in the depths of winter if they are sheltered from the worst of the weather. All of the herbaceous plants illustrated here were flourishing in the ditch by the track leading to the chapel, and many were actually in flower. Ivy covered many of the tree trunks and bore clusters of ripening fruits.

Burdocks, plantains, red deadnettle and the much-branched stems of bristly ox-tongue were also plentiful, and a flock of yellowhammers searched them diligently for seeds.

St Peter's Chapel stands imposingly at the end of the track, exposed to the elements on all four sides and looking out over the North Sea as it has done for thirteen centuries. Built around 654 AD by St Cedd, Bishop of the East Saxons, it is one of the oldest churches in Britain, and it is still occasionally used for services. It stands astride the foundations of the main gateway of the Othona Fort, hence its alternative name of the Chapel of St Peter-on-the-Wall.

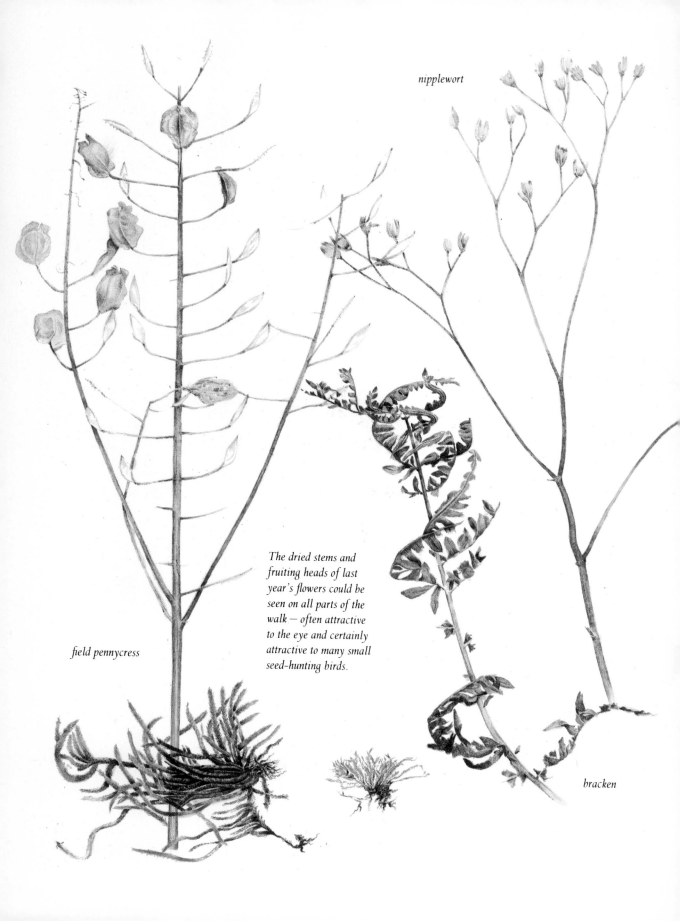

nipplewort

field pennycress

The dried stems and fruiting heads of last year's flowers could be seen on all parts of the walk — often attractive to the eye and certainly attractive to many small seed-hunting birds.

bracken

common reed

sea couch

sea club rush

yarrow

elm

hawthorn

oak

BOVISTA NIGRESCENS:
a fungus

The chapel was built largely with materials from the ruined fort, but a tour of its walls is rather like a geological expedition. The pale brown stones are lumps of clayey limestone derived from the London Clay. They are also known as cement stones or septaria. Most of the light grey stones are pieces of Kentish Rag, a fossil-rich limestone from the Weald of Kent; but there is also, mainly inside the chapel, some tufa limestone from Kent, which has a distinctly honeycombed texture. Here and there in the walls some oolitic limestone can be seen – a rock composed of millions of little rounded limestone grains. St Cedd probably had this brought down from the north-east. Numerous Roman tiles are also incorporated into the building, especially over the arches and in the buttresses. Shell sand was used in the cement bonding, and the shell fragments can easily be seen in the mortar.

The chapel is a plain rectangle today, but it once had a semi-circular chancel at the east end and a tower at the west end. The tower was long used as a beacon. After the chancel was pulled down in the seventeenth century the building was used as a barn, with large doors cut in the north and south walls. It was reconsecrated in 1920 after a good deal of restoration work. The barn doors were bricked up to match the older masonry, but their positions are still quite clear. Far fewer lichens grow on the newer masonry than on the original stones.

The Othona Fort was built during the third century AD and once covered all the ground on the seaward side of the chapel. It was largely destroyed by the Saxons, however, and the North Sea has since swallowed up most of the rest. Excavations have revealed fragments of the fort's walls to the north and south of the chapel, but the only piece visible today is a short section between the chapel and the little cottage now used as a bird observatory.

The desolate saltings, or saltmarshes, beyond the chapel were once used for air-to-ground gunnery practice, and the triangular yellow markers which guided the aircraft towards the targets can still be seen on the thick grey carpet of sea purslane. But the saltings are now at peace, managed as a bird reserve by the Essex Naturalists' Trust. The winding channels of the saltings are filled with water at high tide, but it was low tide as I looked out from the coastal path and the channels were then nothing but muddy grooves decorated with the footprints of hundreds of birds. I could hear the haunting calls of the curlew and the shrill *pic-pic-pic* of the oystercatchers as they flew from one muddy channel to another in search of food; and if I disturbed the oystercatchers they changed their calls to the even shriller *cleep-cleep-cleep*. But the commonest waders on the marsh were the redshanks. The nearest ones stood on the mud and bobbed their heads furiously, indicating that they were suspicious of my presence, and if I moved they took off to loud cries of *duke-duke-duke*. The broad white bar on the hind edge of the wing and the trailing red legs made them easily recognizable as they flew low over the shore.

I turned left at the edge of the saltings and walked along the sea wall, with a spinney of elms shielding me from the stiff off-shore breeze. Sea beet, the ancestor of our cultivated beetroot, is abundant all along the sea wall, its deep green, diamond-shaped leaves springing up from nearly every crevice in company with bristly ox-tongue. The saltings below are dominated by the greyish-leaved sea purslane, while the slightly drier areas support dense clumps of shrubby seablite, identifiable by its succulent leaves which are shaped like miniature sausages. As I passed, flocks of goldfinches and chaffinches were scouring the plants on and around the sea wall in search of seeds.

Immense shell banks rise up beyond the saltings in several places. They cover a vast area, and are some six feet high. When you see them from a distance, it is hard to believe that they are composed entirely of shells, but close examination reveals the truth: millions of shells belonging to cockles, mussels, slipper limpets, oysters, and whelks. Many of the shells are broken, of course, but the appearance of the whelk shells may actually be enhanced by breakage, when their intricate internal coiling is revealed. The shell banks are happy hunting grounds for many birds, and I watched a huge flock of meadow pipits combing one bank for small animals. They took little notice of me, although I was only a few yards away, and then, for no obvious reason, the whole flock was airborne. A few seconds later the reason for their sudden departure came into view, gliding gracefully over the shrubby seablite. It was a short-eared owl, one of the few owls which prefer to hunt by day.

Beyond the saltmarshes and the shell banks stretched oceans of mud, for the tide goes out a long way here. I could just make out the edge of the water, and the shadowy figure of a fisherman digging for lugworms far out beyond St Peter's Chapel. It is, of course, very dangerous to walk out on the mud flats without a good deal of local knowledge, for they can be treacherous in places. The tide also sweeps in very quickly when it turns, running along the creeks and easily cutting off the unwary explorer.

A new stretch of sea wall made walking much easier for a while where the coast begins to swing eastwards into the mouth of the Blackwater, but I had to battle against a strong north-westerly wind. I was not surprised to learn that the Central Electricity Generating Board is considering this wind-swept estuary as a site for a wind-powered generator. Meanwhile, the huge boxes of the nuclear power station loom grimly a little further up the river.

Rows of hefty stakes can be seen stretching out across the mud at low tide. They are the remains of an old groyne system designed to protect the corner from excessive erosion by the tides. Waves lap the sea wall in several places, but the saltings reappear beyond the groynes and form a buffer between the sea and the land. Here I was able to walk on the stabilized banks of shells and shingle, with shrubby seablite growing all

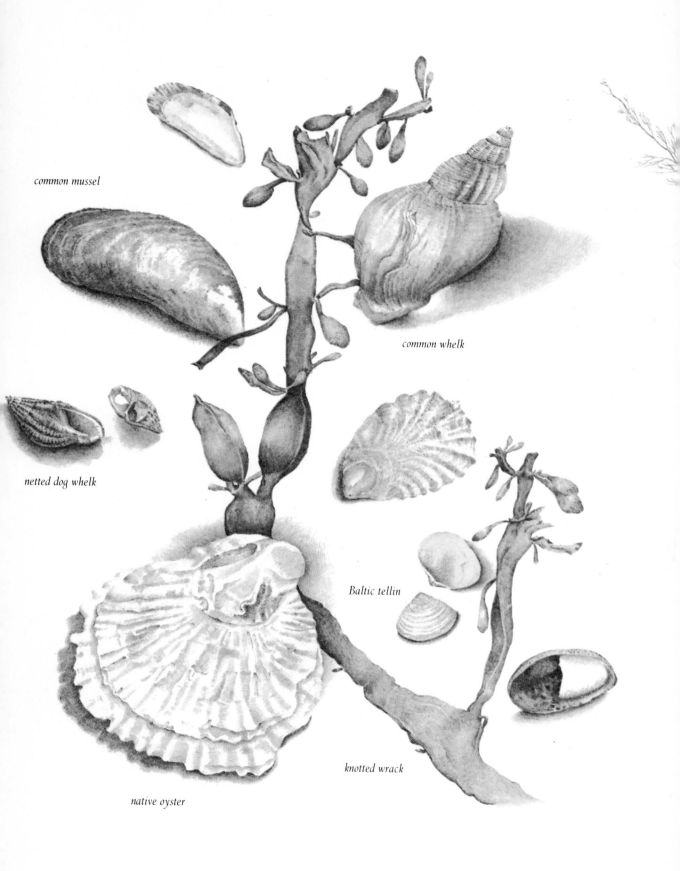

common mussel

common whelk

netted dog whelk

Baltic tellin

native oyster

knotted wrack

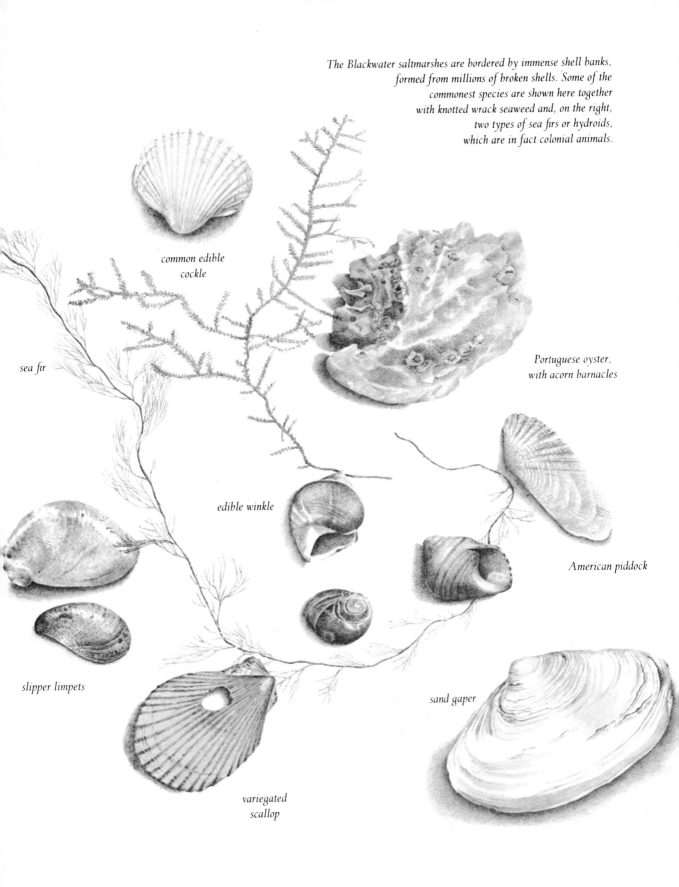

The Blackwater saltmarshes are bordered by immense shell banks, formed from millions of broken shells. Some of the commonest species are shown here together with knotted wrack seaweed and, on the right, two types of sea firs or hydroids, which are in fact colonial animals.

common edible
cockle

sea fir

Portuguese oyster,
with acorn barnacles

edible winkle

American piddock

slipper limpets

sand gaper

variegated
scallop

The Essex coast, with its extensive saltings and numerous muddy
creeks, is a favourite winter haunt of the Brent goose. Little larger
than a mallard, this is our smallest goose, and also the darkest.
It is the only one with an all-black head. It breeds on the Arctic
tundra, but then flies south to spend the winter around the coasts of
Western Europe, normally arriving at about the end of October and
remaining until March. The bird rarely moves far from the coast in
winter, although it sometimes wanders on to the adjacent fields where
it grazes on the winter wheat and barley. Its main feeding places
are the saltings and inter-tidal mud-flats,
where it often occurs in large numbers, flying
low and fast in close formation when disturbed.
Its favourite food is eel-grass, one of the
few kinds of plants that actually grow
in the sea — normally in the inter-tidal
zone. A disease almost wiped out this plant
in Europe during the 1930s and the Brent goose
also became very rare around our coasts, but
both plant and goose have now almost recovered
their former numbers.

around me. On the seaward side, in the muddy pools and creeks of the saltmarsh, I saw many birds, including the Brent geese, who are regular visitors to the Blackwater. I watched several flocks working their way along the winding channels of the saltings. But they are rather shy, and I could not get very close to them: if I approached within about fifty yards the flock took off in unison and, in close formation, flew purposefully away to find a quieter dining room.

I finally lost the saltings just over half a mile to the east of the power station, and then had to choose between the loose shingle of the beach and the muddy path on the sea wall – both rather heavy going. I alternated between the two. The tide was on its way in, and at the water's edge I could see numerous dunlin rushing excitedly to and fro as they examined the debris left by each wave.

The hum of the generators grew louder as I neared the vast buildings of the power station, now silhouetted against the mid-day sun. Out in the estuary stands the stark baffle wall, which controls the supply of cooling water to the reactors and ensures that the discharged warm water is not taken straight back in again. Just after passing the power station I left the sea wall by way of the steep flight of steps leading down to the fields. A flock of lapwings was foraging in stubble, their metallic green upper parts glinting in the sunshine and contrasting beautifully with the clean white 'aprons' which have earned this elegant bird the nick-name 'the butcher'. More lapwings displayed their amazing aeronautic abilities over the adjacent fields.

Following the footpath under some aged willows, I reached the road and kept with it until the sharp left-hand bend. Here I struck off along the footpath between dense lines of hawthorn and blackthorn on the right. I met the road again at the far end of the path and continued towards the village. I was soon crossing the old runway of RAF Bradwell Bay, from which many of the famous wartime Mosquitos – the 'wooden wonders' – took off on their bombing runs over Germany. Bradwell Bay was a very active station, with a wide range of both defensive and offensive roles between 1942 and the end of the war, but it was closed in 1946 and the remaining pieces of runway are now crumbling under a carpet of invading plants. The bright green cushions of biting stonecrop are particularly noticeable to the right of the road, and closer inspection reveals the much smaller, silvery-grey cushions of the silvery thread moss, which fills cracks in the concrete and spills over on to the surface. Yarrow and bristly ox-tongue are the commonest of the larger plants growing here.

A dozen blackbirds disported themselves noisily on the verge as I neared the village indulging in mock fights in between searching the grass for food. Above them, a robin sang first from one side of the road and then from the other, clearly out to tell the world that he owned both sides of the road: what a showman!

The village pump stands by a small white fence on the left of the road. In use until the end of the war, it has recently been restored by the Bradwell Amenities Society, although the water is unfortunately no longer fit to drink. To mark the coronation of Elizabeth II, the Society also provided the school's magnificent wrought iron gates. Bradwell is clearly well looked after by its residents, and as I lunched in The King's Head I could see the Best Kept Village sign standing proudly in the corner of the churchyard. A small lock-up, affectionately known as 'the cage', is built into the churchyard wall, and I can imagine that the humiliation of being penned in there for all to see would have been more than enough punishment for most villains. Cage Row Cottages, some of them neatly weather-boarded, stand attractively behind their tiny front gardens, and just beyond them a real village school, dating from 1727 and an integral part of the village and village life.

I left the village and headed for St Peter's Chapel once more. Out in the open country again, the road is bounded largely by elm hedges, some well trimmed and others sadly neglected. There are also many ancient pollarded elms by the roadside. Some collared doves perched in these trees, and a flock of fieldfares roamed through a lucerne field. Although this field seemed brown and bare from a distance, I could see plump green shoots lurking at the bases of the plants, waiting for the warmth of spring to spark off a new season's growth. The trees around the car park were noisy with starlings, gathering in mid-afternoon before flying off to join thousands of other starlings in a communal roost as much as twenty miles away. We left together as the sun began to set over Bradwell, and the last I saw of them was a tiny black cloud disappearing into the gathering mist.

Winter
FEBRUARY
Thurstaston Common, Merseyside

Thurstaston Common is one of the few remaining wild areas on the Wirral Peninsula. It has escaped cultivation because most of it lies on an exposure of infertile sandstones. Mostly brick-red in colour and rather soft, these rocks belong to a formation known as the Bunter Sands. A harder and less brightly coloured layer of sandstone caps the southern boundary of the common and forms the prominent ridge called Thurstaston Hill, from which there are superb views across the Dee Estuary to the mountains of Snowdonia. The views and the bracing air are enough to make the short climb worthwhile, but there is a great deal more to interest the country-lover who ventures on to Thurstaston Common, even in the middle of winter. The acidic sandy soils support an interesting mixture of heathland and moorland vegetation, with some fine birch woods on the lower and more sheltered slopes. Further variety is contributed by the surrounding parkland, with many splended trees and a wealth of bird life.

Leaving the car park, I made straight for the top of the hill by way of one of the steep paths through the gorse. Rough steps have been carved out of the bright red sandstone by generations of walkers. All around me was the strong, sweet smell of gorse. This spiny shrub is not shy about bringing forth its flowers and it often blooms throughout the winter, although the full flood of yellow is usually held back until the sunny days of April.

Emerging from the gorse, one cannot fail to notice the strong contrast between the dark heather, whose shoots are now virtually purple, and the pale dead leaves of most of the grasses. But life has not deserted the grasses altogether: new shoots and leaves lurk at ground level, just waiting for the warmth of spring to draw them up through the dead leaves and paint the turf green once more. The tall slender flowering stems of the wavy hair grass, which grows mainly on the better drained areas of the common, still stand erect,

The walk is a little over 3 miles long and, except for the initial short climb up from the car park, the route is no more than gently undulating. Parts of it can be very muddy in February, however, and stout, waterproof footwear is recommended. Morning or early afternoon.

Refreshments are not available along the route, but a short detour along the road towards Frankby will take you to the Farmer's Arms.

Cars should be left in the car park by the side of the A540 just north of Thurstaston Church. Map Ref: SJ 247846.

Overleaf: Looking south from Thurstaston Hill, across the Dee to the coast of North Wales. Cloud gathers on the distant mountains and, in the weak February sunshine, Thurstaston's pine trees are silhouetted against the shining waters of the Dee.

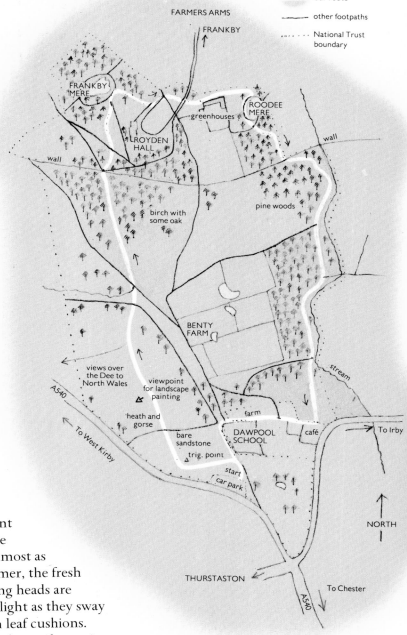

although quite dead, and examination of the delicate heads reveals at once how the plant got its name: the smaller, hair-like branches are exquisitely waved, almost as if they have had a 'perm'. In summer, the fresh stems are reddish and the flowering heads are silvery brown, glinting in the sunlight as they sway elegantly above their bright green leaf cushions.

On most parts of the common the sandstone is covered with peat, but the passage of thousands of human feet has eroded it from the paths. Although basically red, the sandy tracks are stained dark grey

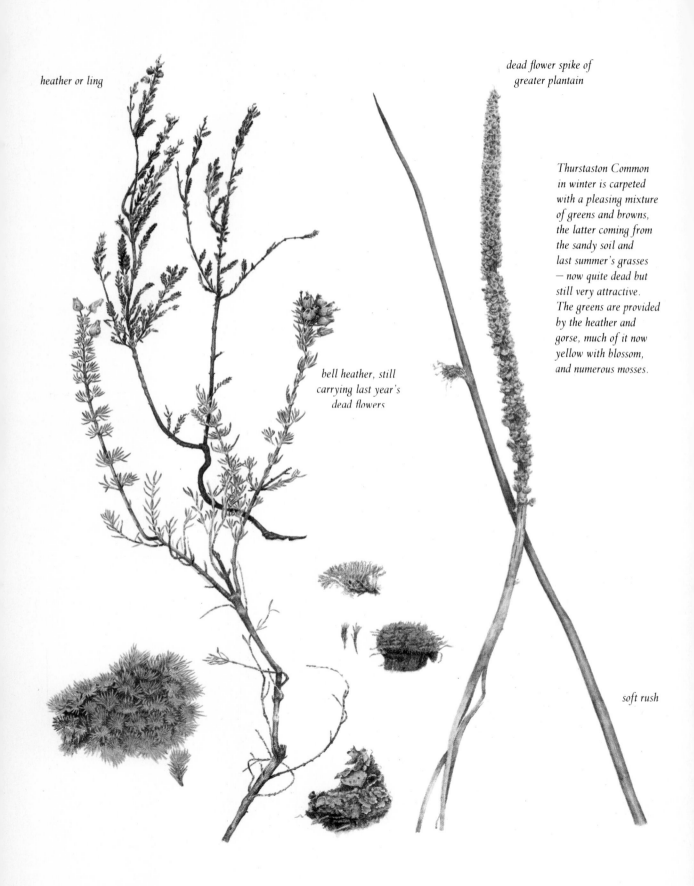

heather or ling

*dead flower spike of
greater plantain*

Thurstaston Common
in winter is carpeted
with a pleasing mixture
of greens and browns,
the latter coming from
the sandy soil and
last summer's grasses
— now quite dead but
still very attractive.
The greens are provided
by the heather and
gorse, much of it now
yellow with blossom,
and numerous mosses.

*bell heather, still
carrying last year's
dead flowers*

soft rush

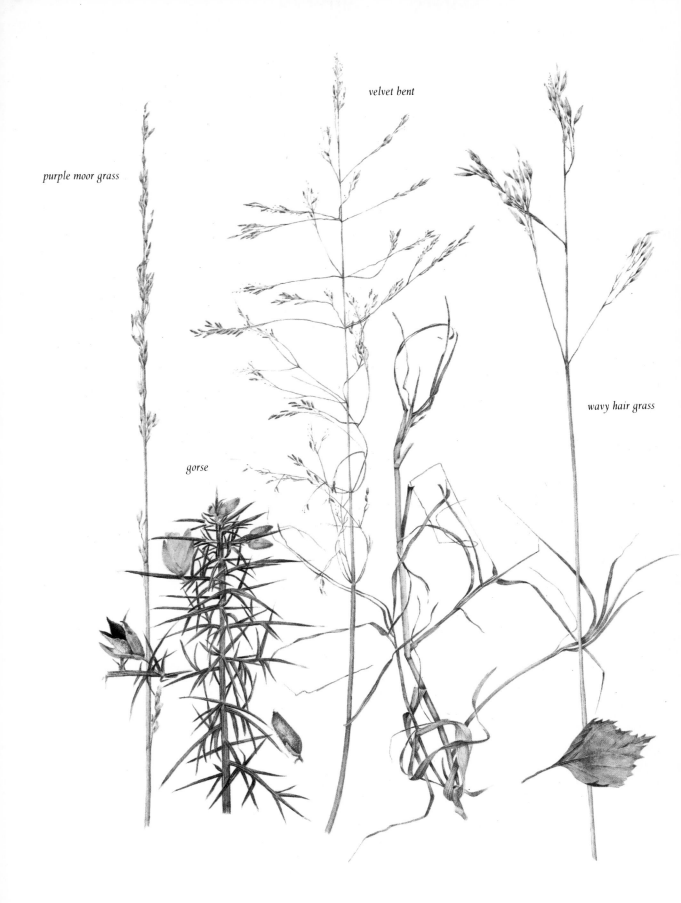

purple moor grass

velvet bent

wavy hair grass

gorse

The bright sandy soil of Thurstaston Hill is clearly
seen here between the gorse and heather.
Beyond the pine trees, flat pastures stretch away to
the banks of the rapidly silting Dee Estuary.

in many places by the peat slurry that flows down them during the winter rains. Erosion is especially marked on the summit, where generations of children have played while their elders have admired the fine views that Thurstaston Hill has to offer. The harder rock, known as the Keuper sandstone, is clearly exposed here, and its fine-grained, layered structure is apparent. The layers, or bedding planes, slope and curve in various directions, indicating that the rocks were originally laid down in shallow moving water – possibly in a delta or at the edge of a lagoon. The concrete pillar standing on these rocks just below the summit is one of the Ordnance Survey's triangulation points used for survey and map-making purposes. The horizontal bench mark engraved on the side of this pillar is approximately 295 feet above sea level, but its height has probably been calculated to within one centimetre!

At the summit of Thurstaston Hill, a little over 300 feet above sea level, an orientation table will help you to identify distant landmarks. To the north, you might see Blackpool Tower and Black Combe in the Lake District, but the finest views are of the Dee Estuary and the Welsh mountains to the south. Snowdonia is visible on a clear day, although this may not augur well for your walk: local residents may even suggest taking your umbrella if you can see Wales, for in the winter months this is often a sign of rain. The estuary is particularly beautiful when the tide is out and the sun is dropping in the west: branching channels show up starkly against its shining surface, and curlews call hauntingly as they seek their evening meals in the mud before the tide returns.

The curlews' calls carry across the flat grazing meadows that stretch out from the river bank – in reality a steep cliff – to the foot of Thurstaston Hill. These meadows lie on poorly drained boulder clays and are dotted with large pools for much of the winter. The boulder clays, which are clearly seen in the riverside cliffs, were deposited by glaciers that swept down from the north during the Ice Age and they contain boulders of granite and other rocks from the Lake District and from Galloway.

Beyond the orientation table, the steep south-facing slope on the left is clothed with a dense growth of heather and gorse. Frequent summer fires, combined with moderate rabbit grazing, keep the plants short. The young gorse shoots here are much greener than the older bushes near the car park. Rabbit tracks and dung heaps are noticeable on the slopes. To the right of the path are a number of damp peaty hollows where Keuper sandstone has been quarried for building. Most of these dry out in summer, leaving only clumps of dark green rushes to mark their sites; but a few pools remain throughout the year on layers of relatively impervious rock. The water is very acidic, however, and contains little animal life.

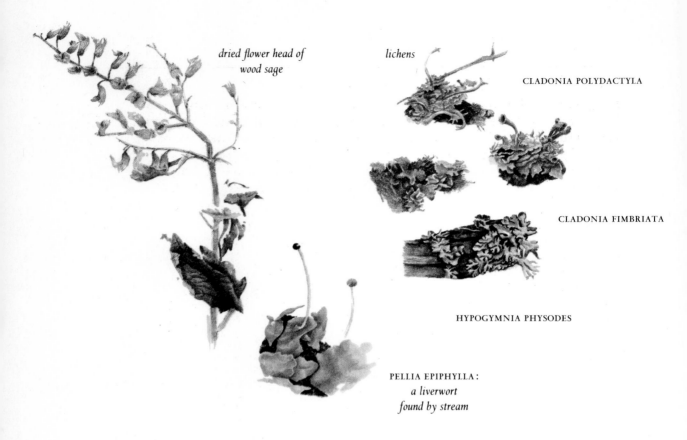

*dried flower head of
wood sage*

lichens

CLADONIA POLYDACTYLA

CLADONIA FIMBRIATA

HYPOGYMNIA PHYSODES

PELLIA EPIPHYLLA:
*a liverwort
found by stream*

Further to the right, and visible only by deviating from the path for a short distance, a huge block of sandstone stands altar-like in the middle of a great crater. Known as Thor's Stone, this rock was once thought to have been carved out by the Vikings for use as a sacrificial altar, but it really owes its existence to its uselessness! Thor's Stone is relatively soft — witness the ease with which hundreds of people have carved their names in it — and unsuitable for building, and it was simply left behind when the surrounding harder rocks were quarried away.

Heather and bilberry are the dominant plants on the plateau and in its numerous hollows, with small patches of bell heather showing up here and there by virtue of its brighter green leaves. Several kinds of mosses occur under the ling and around the rocks. Pixie-cup lichens, looking like minature wine glasses, are common on the peat around the rocks and the bases of the larger plants. There are several species, all belonging to the genus *Cladonia*, and all greyish green and powdery. The powder flakes off easily and each speck can, under the right conditions, grow into a new lichen. Related species, which send up branched or unbranched spikes instead of cups, are also frequent on the peat. They are especially obvious when they produce red spore-bearing patches on their tips.

Hypogymnia physodes is another common lichen, forming rounded grey patches like little doilies on old heather stems. Few lichens grow on the rocks here, but on the vertical surface there are scattered patches of the greyish green *Lecanora conizaeoides*, which looks like crumbly pastry.

The scattered trees on the top of Thurstaston Hill include stark black rowans, identified by their long purplish buds with curved tips, and numerous birches.

A selection of lichens and other plants seen on the heathland and in the woodland. Western hemlock, seen below with an old cone, is one of several introduced trees in the area. It is valued for timber as well as for its attractive conical shape. The mature cone is smooth and egg-shaped, about one inch long.

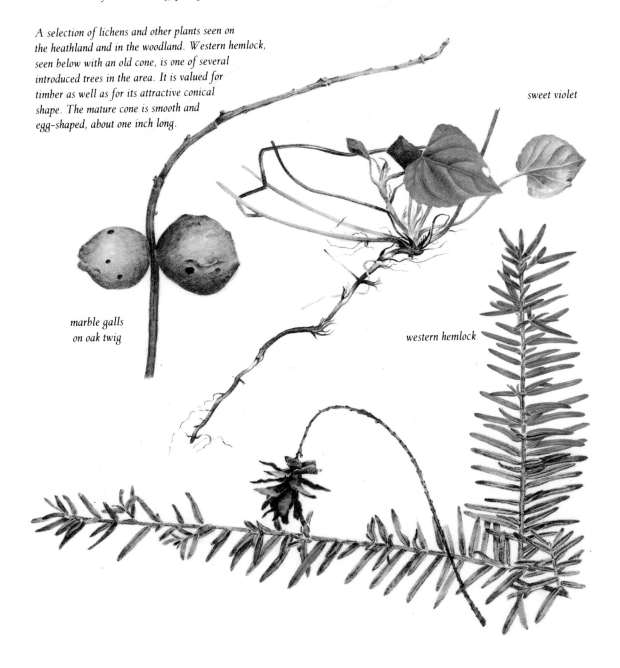

sweet violet

marble galls
on oak twig

western hemlock

There are also plenty of small oaks, many of them bearing brown marble galls on their twigs. These round woody galls grow in the summer around the grub of a small ant-like insect known as a gall wasp. The grub completes its development inside the gall and the adult insect escapes in the autumn. Most of the galls still on the trees in February exhibit neat round exit holes.

I spent some time admiring the aeronautic antics of the many magpies on the common, and then tried to find out just what it was that they were searching for on the ground. It may have been insects around the rabbit droppings, but I found none myself. The jays' digging activities were more easily explained: they were almost certainly unearthing acorns which they had buried during the previous autumn. A single jay has been known to carry more than five thousand acorns from a wood in a month and bury them in different places in the surrounding countryside. Jays also seem to have very good memories, and can find their own acorns even under the snow. But some acorns are obviously unclaimed – hence the young oaks scattered over the common.

I noticed many rooks flying over Thurstaston Hill and the surrounding woodland in search of food and nesting material. They are among the first birds to start nesting, and in late February nest building and repair were already in full swing. The birds were gathering twigs in the tree tops, but also swooped down to collect broken pieces of heather.

Continuing northwards, the path begins to come down off the Keuper capping, and just before entering the birchwood it crosses a small stream running out from the large hollow in the centre of the plateau. The stream, which dries up in the summer, flows over a distinct lip, formed by the lowest of the Keuper beds, and then plunges into a steep gully cut into the softer Bunter sands. The wood contains many beautiful silver birches, and on a sunny day the shining white trunks contrast strongly with the canopy of purple twigs. The male catkins are clearly visible at the tops of the twigs, but they are still firm and compact and must wait a few more weeks before opening out and scattering their pollen in the breeze. The smaller female catkins, which will receive the pollen and form seeds later in the year, are still enclosed in stout buds. They will emerge with the leaves and stand erect on the twigs. Many of the trunks, especially in the upper part of the wood, branch at or very close to the base, probably as a result of damage by fire or rabbits when they were young.

Shelf-like white bracket fungi grow on many of the older trunks. The brackets are just the spore-bearing parts of the fungus, the bulk of which exists as fine threads spreading through the birch tissue. The fungus eventually kills the tree, but it can go on living in the dead wood as well. Mature brackets have a fine corky texture, and entomologists used to collect them and cut them into strips for mounting their insects.

In contrast to many coastal woodlands, the birchwoods of Thurstaston support very few epiphytic lichens on the trunks and branches of the trees. One reason for this is the Wirral's relatively low rainfall: the peninsula lies in the rain shadow of Snowdonia, and the prevailing south-westerly winds have dropped most of their rain before they reach it. Less than thirty inches of rain falls on Thurstaston each year, most of it in the winter, and this is not enough to support the dense, furry lichen growths seen in many other woodlands. But the main reason for the lack of lichens is air pollution from Merseyside and other industrial centres. The epiphytic lichens cannot survive in polluted air. Ground-living lichens are generally less sensitive , but even these cannot live in very polluted areas.

Bracken growing underneath the birches proves that we are still on sandy acidic soil. Although its fronds are now dead, their bright golden colour makes a splendid sight. Bracken does not like cold winds and, although Thurstaston is not particularly windy, the fern is absent from much of the plateau. But it revels in the shade and protection of the birchwood. Numerous mosses grow here as well, and the carpet of dead leaves provides nourishment for a wide variety of autumnal toadstools. During my walk through the birches, I was entertained by the constant ticking and piping of the blue tits, coal tits, great tits, and wrens as they searched high and low for minute specks of insect life. Their chorus was frequently punctuated by the harsh screeching of the jays; and the occasional alarm call of a blackbird — a loud *chook-chook-chook* — warned the other birds that a stranger was in their midst.

At the bottom of the wood, the path meets the old boundary wall of Royden Park. As I crossed into the park, I faced a fine stand of Scot's pine, identifiable by the brick-red upper part of their trunks. I wondered how long they would remain, for the mound on which they grow is a favourite playground for children and soil erosion is very marked. Many of the roots stand far above the present soil surface, and have clearly ceased to anchor the trees in the ground. Wood pigeon nests, little more than rough platforms of twigs, can be seen in the tree tops, together with numerous grey squirrels whose trade-marks are all over the ground in the form of pine cones which have been neatly nibbled to leave just the central core.

Turning right at the pines, I entered a large meadow dotted with mole hills and feeding magpies: again, I could not discover what the birds were eating, but it was probably an assortment of insect grubs in the turf. Many rabbits live here — they often appear grazing on the meadow in late afternoon — but not enough to keep down the tussocks of cocksfoot grass and the inevitable encroachment of birch from the common. The soil in the lower part of this meadow is deeper and richer than anything on the common and may lie on top of a small patch of boulder clay. The earthworms on which the moles feed certainly could not live in the acidic peaty and sandy soils of the common.

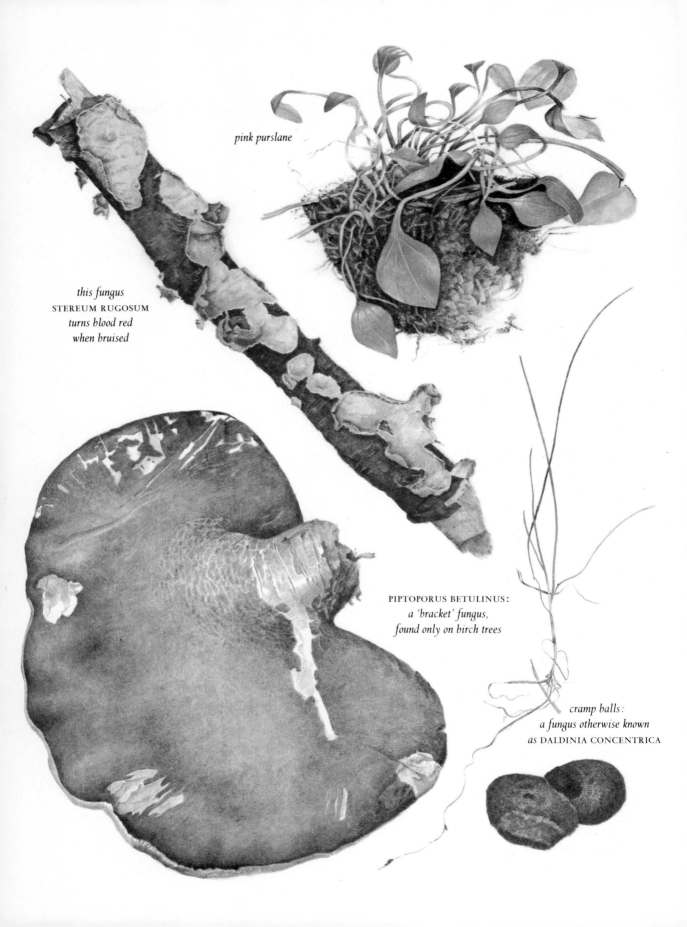

pink purslane

this fungus
STEREUM RUGOSUM
turns blood red
when bruised

PIPTOPORUS BETULINUS:
a 'bracket' fungus,
found only on birch trees

cramp balls:
a fungus otherwise known
as DALDINIA CONCENTRICA

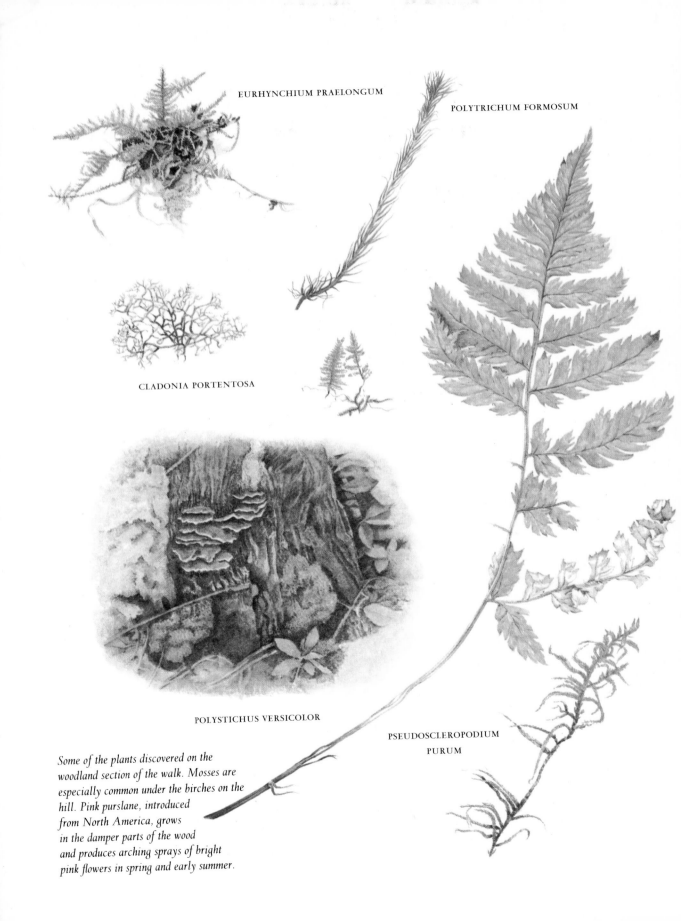

EURHYNCHIUM PRAELONGUM

POLYTRICHUM FORMOSUM

CLADONIA PORTENTOSA

POLYSTICHUS VERSICOLOR

PSEUDOSCLEROPODIUM PURUM

Some of the plants discovered on the
woodland section of the walk. Mosses are
especially common under the birches on the
hill. Pink purslane, introduced
from North America, grows
in the damper parts of the wood
and produces arching sprays of bright
pink flowers in spring and early summer.

The path skirts the bottom of the meadow, keeping the pines and an assortment of introduced trees on the left. The exotic trees often planted in parks and gardens certainly add splendour to the landscape – usually with bright flowers and leaves. In the case of the madrona tree (*Arbutus menziesii*), however, it is the bark which provides colour. The outer layer peels away from the branches revealing bright orange-red patches beneath. A fine specimen of this evergreen tree, which is native to western North America, overhangs the lower edge of the meadow, but it is unusual in having toothed leaves.

Just beyond the madrona tree lies a small pond. It usually dries out in summer, as might be guessed from the sallows and other shrubs growing in the middle, but it is now a haven for birds. Wrens and blue tits were busily searching for insects among the bare branches as I walked by. From here the path rises gently beside the rhododendrons, and on the left grow more small oaks, including the Turkey oak. This differs from the common species in having longer and more deeply-cut leaves – some were still clinging to the branches of these trees – and also in having rather shaggy or whiskery buds. Its acorn cups are also shaggy. Although not introduced to Britain until the middle of the eighteenth century, the Turkey oak is now widely distributed and represented by some very large specimens.

Foxes make their home in this wooded part of the park, and their strong musky smell is noticeable in places where they habitually cross the path on their way to chase rabbits in the meadow. Look for their footprints in the soft ground, but don't confuse them with the prints of the numerous dogs that are walked through the park: the fox's footprint is narrower than that of most dogs, with more slender claw marks, and it also has a much larger gap between the main pad and the two central toe pads.

Keeping to the left of the buildings at the top of the path, I stopped to admire the fascinating witch hazel, an introduced shrub whose wispy brown and yellow flowers were in full bloom on the otherwise bare branches. I then turned right along the narrow path through the rhododendrons to find a large, tree-fringed lake with beautiful reflections. Alder trees, with their old, cone-like catkins still on their branches, make fine frames through which to view this tranquil scene; but the silence is often broken by bursts of what sounds like machine-gun fire. After the initial shock, I realized that I was listening to great spotted woodpeckers hammering against the tree trunks. This activity, known as drumming, serves to indicate ownership of a territory. You may well hear a burst of drumming from one clump of trees, and then a reply from another. A pair of binoculars may pick out the colourful birds in the trees on the far side of the lake or in the nearby pines. Specially toughened skulls ensure that the birds come to no harm through their rapid hammering, and it is interesting that scientists have recently studied the structure of the woodpecker skull in an attempt to design safer crash-helmets for motor cyclists.

I crossed the park boundary again and walked through the pines. Abundant saplings show that the trees are setting plenty of seed and that the squirrels are not devouring it all. The pines gradually thin out on the lower ground and are replaced by scrubby oaks and numerous birches. The latter again carry many bracket fungi. Towards the margin of the wood, the path crosses on to the heavy boulder clay and the ground becomes very wet. It remains wet even in summer, as a result of the water draining out of the neighbouring sandstone. I turned right at the margin of the wood and followed the path more or less parallel to the edge. Brambles are abundant here, where plenty of light reaches the ground. A small stream flows along the margin of the wood and its sticky, clay banks are here and there clothed with dense mats of the liverwort known as *Pellia.* This looks like a dark green seaweed, but it is actually more closely related to the mosses. Careful examination at this time of year will reveal spherical black capsules on the surface. These will soon grow up on pale stalks and split open to release spores. The pale inner surfaces are exposed when the capsules open, and the whole plant appears to be covered with tiny stars.

The flat wet ground is studded with large tussocks of purple moor grass. Draped with dead leaves, these are almost white in the winter, but new green leaves will appear in the spring and be followed by the delicate purple flower heads. In fact the grass does not flower too well in this shady habitat. It likes wet places, but only where the water flows slowly through or over the ground: it does not tolerate stagnant water. The path gradually rises again, and soon emerges from the wood. Clumps of bracken, broom, and gorse indicate that we are back on sandstone. After crossing the stile at the corner of School Lane and noticing its sturdy sandstone pillars, I turned right and walked along the lane to the bottom of Thurstaston Hill. The contrast between the heather and the grass is again very marked, and golden bracken also decorates this more sheltered slope of the hill. Tufts of purple moor grass grow on the sides of the erosion gullies, although the tufts are much smaller than those in the wood. Turning left at the school, the track skirts the bottom of the hill, through more gorse bushes, and returns to the car park.

INDEX
of species illustrated

Hardheads (black knapweed): *Centaurea nigra* 100, 101
Harebell: *Campanula rotundifolia* 100
Hart's-tongue fern: *Asplenium scolopendrium* 20
Hawthorn: *Crataegus monogyna* 117, 173
Hazel catkin: *Corylus avellana* 17
Heather (ling): *Calluna vulgaris* 186
Hedgehog: *Erinaceus europaeus* 102
Herb robert: *Geranium robertianum* 48
Heron: *Ardea cinerea* 67
Highland cow: *bos tauros* 145
Hookeria lucens 30
Hops: *Humulus lupulus* 119
Hydra: *Hydra viridissima* 53
Hygrophorus 111

Indian balsam: *Impatiens glandulifera* 121
Ivy, common: *Hedera helix* 170
Ivy, ground: *Glechoma hederacea* 171

Kestrel: *Falco tinnunculus* 19
Knotted wrack: *Asophyllum modosum* 64, 176

Lady's mantle: *Alchemilla vulgaris* 100
Larch, common: *Larix decidua* 146
Large skipper butterfly: *Ochlodes venatus* 79
Lesser celandine: *Ranunculus ficaria* 21
Lesser periwinkle: *Vinca minor*, 37
Lichens: *Cladonia floerkeana*, *Cladonia squamosa* 148; *Cladonia fimbriata*, *Cladonia polydactyla*, *Hypogymnia physodes* 190
Light crottle lichen: *Ochrolechia parella* 22
Ling *see* heather
Liverwort: *Pellia epiphylla* 190; *Lunularia cruciata* 35
Lousewort: *Pedicularis sylvatica* 68
Lycoperdon perlatum 111

Maple, field: *Acer campestre* 136
Meadow cranesbill: *Geranium pratense* 79
Meadow pipit: *Anthus pratensis* 63
Mermaid's purse of dogfish: *Scyliorhinus caniculus* 64
Moschatel: *Adoxa moschatel* 16
Mushroom, field: *Agaricus campestris* 115
Mussel, common: *Mytilus edulis* 176

Navelwort: *Umbilicus rupestris* 22
Netted dog whelk: *Nassarius reticulatus* 176

Newt, smooth: *Triturus vulgaris* 68
Nipplewort: *Lapsana communis* 172

Oak: *Quercus* spp. 173
Old man's beard *see* traveller's joy
Orchid, heath spotted: *Dactylorhiza ericetorum* 69
Otter shell, common: *Lutraria lutraria* 177
Oyster, native: *Ostrea edulis* 176; Portuguese: *Crassostrea angulata* 177
Oystercatcher: *Haematopus ostralegus* 67

Painted lady butterfly: *Cynthia cardui* 96
Pennybun boletus: *Boletus edulis* 114
Pennycress, field: *Thlaspi arvense* 172
Peppermint: *Mentha* x *piperata* 82
Petty spurge: *Euphorbia peplus* 170
Pixie-cup lichen: *Cladonia pyxidata* 14
Plagiomnium undulatum 30
Polytrichum commune 31
Primrose: *Primula vulgaris* 16
Purple moor grass: *Molinia caerulea* 187

Rabbit: *Oryctolagus cuniculus* 80, 81
Ramsons (wild garlic): *Allium ursinum* 21, 31
Red campion: *Silene dioica* 36
Red dead nettle: *Lamium purpureum* 171
Red deer: *Cervus elaphus* 152, 153
Reed, common: *Phragmites communis* 173
Reed canary grass: *Phalaris arundinacea* 151
Robin: *Erithacus rubecula* 117
Rosehip: *Rosa canina* 118
Rowan: *Sorbus aucuparia* 104
Russula fragilis 110

Sallow: *Salix caprea* 163; grey willow: *Salix cinerea* 31
Sandhopper: *Orchestia gammarella* 65
Scallop, variegated: *Chlamys varia* 177
Scentless mayweed: *Tripleurospermum maritimum inodorum* 170
Sea anemone: *Actinia equina* 65
Sea club rush: *Scirpus maritimus* 173
Sea couch: *Agropyron redens* 173
Sea fir 177
Sea pink *see* thrift
Shepherd's purse: *Capsula bursa-pastoris* 171
Shrimp, freshwater: *Gammarus pulex* 53, 82
Silverweed: *Potentilla anserina* 48
Sitka spruce: *Picea sitchensis* 147